Blessings,
Carolyn Carter

# One MORE Heartbeat

*Chosen to receive God's Miracles*

**CAROLYN CARTER**

WestBow
PRESS
A DIVISION OF THOMAS NELSON

WestBow Press books may be ordered through booksellers or by contacting:

WestBow Press
A Division of Thomas Nelson
1663 Liberty Drive
Bloomington, IN 47403
www.westbowpress.com
1-(866) 928-1240

Because of the dynamic nature of the Internet, any web addresses or links contained in this book may have changed since publication and may no longer be valid. The views expressed in this work are solely those of the author and do not necessarily reflect the views of the publisher, and the publisher hereby disclaims any responsibility for them.

Any people depicted in stock imagery provided by Thinkstock are models, and such images are being used for illustrative purposes only.

Certain stock imagery © Thinkstock.

ISBN: 978-1-4497-3935-5 (sc)
ISBN: 978-1-4497-3936-2 (hc)
ISBN: 978-1-4497-3934-8 (e)

Library of Congress Control Number: 2012901997

Printed in the United States of America

WestBow Press rev. date: 02/14/2012

# CONTENTS

# DEDICATION

First and foremost I dedicate the words in this book to my Lord and Savior, who has been so faithful in answering the many prayers I have voiced throughout my life. I am humbled by the miracles in my life that have been a gift from You, and I thank You, Lord, for letting me share Your love and provision for me with others.

I also dedicate this book to my loving husband, Gary, who has stood by my side for forty-one wonderful years of marriage. Your love has been reflected in your support through life-altering decisions and life-changing health issues. Thank you for the high standards you set for our two sons, Chris and Tim. Their marriages are strong because of your example of love for me as your wife. Now they are fathers setting the same loving example in their own homes.

I also dedicate this book to our sons, Chris and Tim, who have always made our lives exciting and full of love and laughter. Thank you, Chris, for allowing me to share some of the harder times of your life in this book. I pray that the words herein may bless others and result in a strengthening of their faith when they have trying times. Chris and Tim, I love you both dearly and am proud of the men you have become.

I also dedicate this book to my two prayer partners, Beth Fitts and Rosemary Brewer. You both are awesome friends. Our weekly prayer times for more than twenty years have taught me how to pray and then to be patient while waiting for God's response. Our prayer times followed by a steaming cup of coffee have bonded a friendship that I will cherish always. (If I had a nickel for each cup of coffee we have had together, I would be a rich woman today.)

And I dedicate this book to a wonderful friend and doctor, Jeff Evans. Along with our Lord Jesus Christ, you truly are my hero. I have you to thank for both saving my life and restoring my health. Without a doubt, you were a major part of a present-day miracle of God. I thank you for not giving up when the chips were down.

# PREFACE

When you look out over a roaring crowd at a football game, what do you see? You see garments drenched in school colors, large, swaying pom-poms, some open mouths shouting praises to their team, and some mouths clenched with disapproval for a play gone bad.

But can you see into the hearts of the people in the crowd? No—but God can. He doesn't just look at their clothes and faces; He looks into their hearts. He knows their hearts and their talents and how best to use each one.

I have often wondered when God was passing out beautiful voices, why I wasn't chosen. I have also wondered why I wasn't chosen to paint beautiful artwork that would grace the walls of homes around the world. For a long time, I spent a lot of time feeling abandoned by God when the talents were handed out.

And then, through the experiences in my life, I realized that God saw something different in my heart and my future. He saw a heart that wanted to share His love with others. He saw a heart that loved Him and wanted others to know how wonderful it really is to be a believer in Jesus Christ.

God has chosen me to show His mercy and provision in another way—in a way that I never imagined. He has been writing the chapters of my life in a way that He knew someday would become the events and miracles shared with others through a book. In *One More Heartbeat,* I share the many ways God has walked beside me and performed miracles that can be explained in no other way.

The characters in my book are family members and friends, everyday people just like you and me. When the miracles were performed, I'm sure that others heard no whistles blowing and saw no flags waving—but I did. My family and friends have been used as instruments to bring these acts of provision into reality. I acknowledge that I have felt the earth move several times and that I have been the recipient of more than my share of the grace of almighty God.

I hope you will feel the same moving of the earth and hear the same whistles blowing as you read this book. I wrote it for the glory of God and to let others know that God is with us at all times. He will answer your prayers if you are willing to rely totally on Him. Sometimes that may require patience. You may think He is not listening, but be assured that He is and knows your heart and your future. He will answer in a way that is best for you.

I hope and pray that you are blessed as you read *One More Heartbeat*.

# CHAPTER 1

# BLIND DATES—
# THE GOOD, THE BAD, AND THE UGLY

I have been absolutely awed by the answers that I have received to my prayers. I have enjoyed a wonderful, open relationship with the Lord and trusted Him for guidance daily since the age of thirteen. Sometimes my prayers are not answered quickly and I have to be patient and wait. However, just anticipating how God will see fit to answer is so exciting. I have kept a journal of my prayer requests, and when I look back through it, I can see that some prayers were answered on the same day I prayed them while others may have been answered years later. However, God has always answered my prayers in His perfect timing and not in mine. He has taught me how to wait upon Him, for He knows my future.

Back in my college days, while I was attending Ole Miss and living on campus, God gave me peace and guidance many times about who to date, what parties to attend, and which ones to stay away from. I always felt His presence when I was teased or ridiculed for not drinking at parties, not missing curfew, and not getting into a car with a drunk driver.

On one particular blind date, my date and I doubled-dated for a cookout at Sardis Lake. The night was so much fun, but I quickly realized that not only was my date drunk, but everyone around me was also drunk. I was the only sober person on the beach. What a problem!

We were twenty miles away from the campus at 11:30 p.m., and curfew was at midnight. I really needed to leave, but no one was sober but me, so how was I going to get back to campus? I was beginning to realize what a naïve, sheltered girl I had been. I had not grown up around people who drank, nor had I ever had to deal with drunk people before.

I thought this was a great time to ask for the Lord's help and guidance in this very touchy situation. I believe God knows what we are thinking even before we speak, so I just raised my eyes to the heavens and prayed silently. I needed help! I asked God to give me wisdom and the right words to say when I confronted my date, who was also the driver, about our trip back to campus. Then God gave me a boldness I had never felt before. I had always been a follower, and my shy nature had always prevented me from stepping into a leadership role. I was happy never to have had a confrontational moment, but I was afraid I was about to have one.

I looked around for my date and found him sitting in the wet sand. He had a beautiful quilt his mom had made for him around his head. He had cut a huge gash in the center of the quilt and was wearing it like a poncho. I knew he would regret that decision in the morning, but I didn't have time to worry about that now. I calmly asked if I could see the keys to his car, and much to my surprise, he handed them to me.

I found the other couple who rode to Sardis with us sitting at a picnic table, giggling and drinking. I "escorted" them to the car and put them in the backseat. After they were buckled in, I went back for my date. Without resistance, he followed me to the car and got in on the passenger side. Then I got behind the wheel of the most beautiful red sports car I had ever seen or driven. By this time, it was 11:40 p.m., and we only had twenty minutes to get back to campus. I had always been a very reliable driver. I never drove too fast, never ran red lights, always signaled before turning, and had a squeaky clean driving record. But I needed to get back to campus fast, so I put the pedal to the metal and drove almost ninety all the way back.

We drove up in front of the dormitory at 11:56. I had made it! Now the question was what should I do with the three drunk people who were passed out in the car? I shook them and called their names. I opened the car doors to let cool air into the car, but nothing woke them up! The only thing I could think of to do was to lock the doors and let them sleep it off in front of my dormitory. I walked inside, said goodnight to the dorm mother, and went to bed.

Needless to say, my drunk date never asked me out again, which certainly pleased me. I did regret that the girl in the car never really considered me a friend anymore, but I had cut down my list of friends who liked to drink. That night I redefined my expectations for future dates.

I dated lots of different types of guys in college—some who were handsome, some who were not. Some of them were outgoing and some were shy. I remember one guy who I was convinced had a bullfrog in his family tree. He was short and round and had big, round, bulging eyes. Then there was the guy who had blue lips. I was sure he had some medical disorder, so I never went out with him again. These were mixed in with guys who could have been on the cover of a fashion magazine. I enjoyed meeting so many really nice people, but I never found Mr. Right.

At the beginning of my senior year at Ole Miss, Peggy, one of my sorority sisters, called and asked if I had plans for Friday night. She said that a friend of hers needed a date for a beach party at Sardis. Well, needless to say, that set off the alarm in my brain. I immediately said no. She said that her friend's date had cancelled, and he really wanted to attend this party. She assured me that he was not going to drink. She also assured me that she would be at the party and would be available for a ride home if I needed one. Reluctantly, I agreed to go. She told me that my date would be Gary Carter.

Uh oh! I had met Gary and was not impressed with him at all. Hurricane Camille hit the Mississippi Gulf Coast on August 17, 1969. The coast was totally destroyed, and the residents needed help of all kinds. My mother belonged to the Pilot Club of Oxford, and the club had planned a roadblock for Hurricane Camille victims about two weeks after the hurricane hit to collect money for the devastated people who lived to the south of us. She asked me if I would like to get several of my friends to stand at the roadblock and help collect money, so I asked my friends Peggy, Becky, and Lee. We were excited to help raise money for such a worthy cause.

We had a ball standing in the street, stopping cars, and we asked for any donations the drivers could offer. The donations surpassed our expectations, and the afternoon was a total success. Just before we were getting ready to complete our collections, a young man walked up to Peggy, and they talked for a while. Then she brought him over to us. Peggy introduced Gary as her friend and said that he had walked into town to get warm.

Apparently the air conditioning in his dorm was stuck, and the building was frigid. I could have explained to him why he was so cold if only he had asked! He was wearing blue-jean cutoffs that had raveled up so short that the pockets were showing below the frayed bottoms. I was embarrassed to look at him—but he did have a great personality and was very outgoing.

None of the other girls seemed bothered by his short cutoffs, but I thought they looked awful. My mother and some of the other Pilot Club members were helping at the same roadblock, and I dreaded their reactions to Gary's shorts. I saw my mother coming over to me with a purpose-driven look on her face. Her forthcoming comments were surely going to be about this boy and his chosen attire!

Much to my surprise, my mother suggested that I invite my friends to our house for a Coke. Our house was just about a block away, so we could walk and take a break there. The comment that surprised me the most was when my mother said, "Carolyn, be sure to invite that nice young man too!"

Well, he heard her, and I was doomed! I had to invite him too, and I didn't want to at all. We all left the roadblock and enjoyed a quick snack at my house. Gary was cute and did have a great personality, but I was totally grossed out by his shorts. It would have been fine with me if I never saw him again.

Well, about a week after our roadblock, the time for our Sardis date was growing closer. Peggy assured me that Gary would not wear the cutoffs and that I would have a great time. I dreaded the date all week but couldn't figure out a way to get out of it. At 6:30 on Friday night, I was ready and waiting when the telephone rang in my sorority house room. The caller said, "Hi, this is Gary, and I'm here to pick you up."

Still dreading the night, I left my room, locked the door, and walked down to the chapter room in the sorority house. Gary was standing there anxiously awaiting my arrival. I quickly realized that maybe I was not the only one who was disappointed about the date. His real date had cancelled, and I was a substitute. But we were going to make the best of the evening. I have to admit that he looked good. He was all cleaned up and had on real clothes. He was very polite and kept the conversation moving along, which made me feel more and more comfortable.

Gary was funny and lots of fun to be with. Everyone at the party knew him and obviously thought he was a great guy. We had so much fun that I quickly forgot I had not wanted to go out with him.

We talked and talked and seemed to have everything in common. I started to really like this guy! After a fun evening, we got back to the sorority house just a few minutes before curfew. We talked for a few minutes at the front door, and he told me he had enjoyed the evening. He smiled, turned around, and walked to his car. I was shocked! This guy must be from outer space, I thought, because all college boys would try to kiss you good night, even on a first date. Gary had not! Oh no, I liked him, and I thought he must not like me. Now I was afraid that he would not ask me out again.

But after that night, neither Gary nor I dated anyone else. We talked or went out every night. My sorority sisters teased us because they said we looked alike, thought alike, and were always smiling when we were together. Yes, I definitely was falling in love, and Gary was too. I assumed this must be from God because we seemed so perfectly matched and were so deeply in love. I never once stopped to ask God if this was His plan for my mate. By that time, I would not have wanted to hear the answer God might have given me unless it was yes.

Gary was not a Christian. His family had attended the Presbyterian church in Laurel, since he was a little boy. He knew about God but had never accepted Him as his Lord and Savior. Gary was a great, great guy. He was polite, respectful, and very devoted to me and my family. My parents loved him like a son. He asked me to marry him the May after our first date, and I immediately accepted. Still, I never once thought to ask God about His perfect plan for my life. We planned the wedding for an August evening, which just happened to be a little over a year after Hurricane Camille hit the Gulf Coast. What a coincidence! The summer was spent ordering invitations, picking out dresses, choosing cakes, and all the other things involved in making our day perfect.

With all of the planning done, the big day finally came. The weather was beautiful, the church was breathtaking, and the attendants were all jittery and ready. The ceremony couldn't have been more perfect. We were married and ready to start our "perfect" life together.

But within just a few months following our big day, I began to see things in Gary's personality I had not seen before. He would have a beer once in a while, but never anything stronger. I decided I could live with that even though I didn't drink at all. He also began to show a temper that apparently had been suppressed while we were dating.

I will admit now that we really didn't know each other as well as we should have. We dated for a year but were apart for much of that time. We began dating in September, but I moved to Clarksdale for three months of student teaching in that same month. We saw each other on weekends but not during the week. I was home by the second week in December, and we saw each other daily during that month. When January came, Gary went off to basic training until May 1. We wrote letters to each other almost daily, but I only saw him once during those months. We really had not had enough time to get to know each other. He asked me to marry him about three weeks after his return from Fort Polk. I admit that this did not throw any warning signs out to me. I was sure we were in love and would be happy forever.

I realized in the short time we were married that I needed to confess to God that I might have made a mistake. I had not prayed for His guidance at all before making this lifelong decision. I didn't want to admit it because I still loved Gary tremendously. Still, I confessed that I had been wrong not to seek God's will in this very important decision. I wanted our marriage to work, so I prayed for patience and for God to work a miracle in Gary's heart.

I did not always let Gary see me praying because I was afraid he might make fun of me. When I wanted to attend church, he would sometimes say I loved that church more than I loved him. He felt I should stay home with him on Sunday and enjoy the day off. I couldn't explain to Gary that I truly did love God more than I loved him because Gary would never understand. Only a Christian can understand the love, protection, and support that only God can give. I prayed earnestly for Gary's salvation.

I had to face the fact that because we were unequally yoked, our marriage might not make it, but I was determined to make it work if there was anything I could do with God's help.

I began to check Gary's attitude on Sunday morning and attend church when he didn't seem to mind. I also thanked God for my food before each meal in a silent way. I knew God understood my situation. I wanted to be as patient and understanding as a Christian can be.

I will admit that many times I have charged ahead of God and tried to solve problems by myself or make decisions without even considering that I should ask God first. God has been very gracious in teaching me through my mistakes and disobedience that He is still there with me even though I may have forgotten to consult Him about my decisions.

I remember one example that taught me not only to ask for guidance first but also to be submissive to my sweet husband, even though he was not a Christian. We had an old refrigerator that had a small freezer on the top. I loved to can and freeze fresh vegetables in the summer. Nothing tastes better in the winter than homegrown butterbeans, black-eyed peas, and corn. Later, when the children were young, I even attempted a garden in a vacant lot behind an apartment complex Gary and I owned. I became quite a gardener and was pleased when I could harvest the results of all my hard work.

Now I had decided that we needed an upright freezer so I would have a place to store all my treasured frozen vegetables from the summer harvest. I asked Gary about buying a freezer, and he immediately said, "We can't afford one right now."

I knew that, but I wanted one anyway and I wanted it *now*. I thought and thought about how I could get a freezer. Then I had a plan! I decided that I would save a little out of my paycheck each week and put it in an envelope in my lingerie drawer. After all, nobody goes into a lady's lingerie drawer but her. Well, several months went by, and I had saved up $400. I decided that the time had come to go to the appliance store and see what they had. I still had not shared my plan with Gary.

On my day off, I went to the store and told my cousin Ed, who owned the store, that I had $400 and wanted to buy an upright freezer. He had just the perfect one. We agreed that I would come back after lunch to pay him, and then he would have the freezer delivered by

4:00 p.m. I was so excited, and I knew Gary would be too when he found out I had saved up the money for the freezer.

My mother had invited us to her house for lunch that day. On the way, I told Gary about my plan. I was expecting him to be thrilled that I had been such a skilled saver, but I was devastated when he said to call the store and tell them to cancel my order for the freezer. I begged him and tried to explain how proud he should be of me instead of making such a harsh demand. He stood fast and insisted that I call the store as soon as lunch was over.

We arrived at my parents' house and pulled into the driveway. I begrudgingly got out of the car and went into the house. I acted like nothing had happened because I didn't want my parents to worry that Gary and I were fighting. We had a wonderful lunch of roast, black-eyed peas, fresh fried corn, and cornbread. Mother had baked a warm pound cake for dessert. But all of her delicious food didn't do anything to improve my desire for that wonderful, white upright freezer.

After lunch, we got into the car to go back to work. I had left my purse on the floor in the front seat, and I noticed that it was not where I had left it. It was sitting on the seat instead of on the floor. I immediately opened my purse, and my wallet was missing, along with my checkbook, my driver's license, my credit cards, and the $400 I had saved. I was devastated!

Gary sensed my disappointment and embarrassment and said, "Carolyn, I am very sorry. I know how much you wanted a freezer." He never said, "I told you so." He knew I had learned my lesson.

But what could I do? I needed to stop payment on my checks, cancel my credit cards, and get another driver's license. I had so much to do. When I was thinking about all the things I had lost, I realized that some precious baby pictures of our two boys were also in my wallet, and those could not be replaced.

With a feeling of total despair, I realized that I needed to ask God for guidance. I needed to admit I had been a more than a little headstrong and that I needed to let Gary be the head of our household. I needed to ask forgiveness and then turn this problem over to the One who could help me make the correct decisions and solve this problem. I called the store and cancelled my big plan to buy a new freezer. That night, I asked Gary to forgive me, and then I began to pray. I asked God to help me find my wallet. I really didn't care anymore about the money. I just wanted my pictures back.

The next morning after opening up the jewelry store and getting ready for the day, I got a call from an employee of our local newspaper. He said he was coming in to work and found my wallet by the dumpster behind his office. All of my pictures, my credit cards, my driver's license, and my checkbook were still in my wallet. I asked if there was any money in the wallet, and he quietly replied, "No."

I didn't care. I had learned two wonderful lessons so early in my marriage and had been rewarded with the things that really mattered. God had allowed a friend to find my wallet and answered my prayer. God is good!

# CHAPTER 2

# THE WONDERFUL
# LITTLE COUNTRY CHURCH

About two years after Gary and I were married, our first son, Chris, was born. We were so excited! Our little bundle of joy had arrived, and we never dreamed what a life-changing event having a baby can be. He arrived about six weeks before he supposedly was due. We had even ridden our bicycle built for two to work the day before his birth, never knowing things were about to change our lives so soon.

I worried and worried that Chris might be a tiny baby and unable to make it because he was born so early. When the doctor told me that he weighed nine pounds, ten ounces, I accused him of lying to me. I was afraid that he just didn't want me to worry. Gary came into the room and assured me that Chris was fine. He would start off his little life in three to six month sizes and would be just fine.

When Chris was born, fathers were not allowed to see their babies except through the nursery window until the day the baby was to go home from the hospital. The hospital actually had a red velvet rope strung up across the hallway to prevent anyone from entering the mother's room while the baby was there.

Gary would look at Chris through the nursery window but was not allowed to hold him. While he was looking through the nursery window at Chris on the afternoon he was born, another new dad walked up beside him. They were admiring their babies, and the other dad said, "Wow, I'd love to meet the daddy of that baby. He is huge!" Gary turned to the guy, stuck his hand out, and said, "Hi, I'm Gary Carter, and that's my son." Gary himself is not all that big. At the time, he was five-foot-eight and weighed about 165. We still don't know where Chris got his size because I was not a big person either!

Gary was scheduled to leave for a two-week national guard summer camp at Camp Shelby on Friday after Chris was born on Thursday. He called everyone he could think of but was unable to leave for camp any later. He would have to be gone for two weeks without getting to welcome his first child into the world and hold him in his arms.

I decided to stay with my parents while Gary was gone. They had Mamie, a chubby little black lady who had helped raise both my brother and me. Mamie never had any children of her own but had worked for our family since my brother was three years old, which was two years before I was born. I knew Mamie would know what to do, and I was scared to death I would do something wrong. Between my mother and Mamie, I learned how to take care of a baby in those two weeks Gary attended summer camp.

After Gary got home and we became a family, I was sure our life would be perfect, but things only became more tense at times. Chris was not a settled baby and often cried at night. On some nights I would get up five or six times. I was working all day and not getting enough sleep at night. We had a wonderful family support system. My parents lived two houses down from us and would often call and offer to pay for our supper and a movie if they could keep Chris. This was a saving grace and allowed Gary and me to have some time alone.

Gary resented the Sundays when I got up and wanted to take Chris to church. I had attended church alone since we got married and wanted to continue attending. I wanted Chris to be exposed to the Word of God and have a firm foundation when the time came for him to accept Christ as his Lord and Savior. Gary questioned why we couldn't spend the day together as a family instead of being split up between church and home. He was not interested in attending with us at all.

Gary had a quick temper, which showed its face on many Sunday mornings. He would lose his temper often and occasionally throw things across the room. He broke several dishes on the floor right in front of Chris's high chair. I knew something had to be done, so I prayed harder that God would open Gary's heart and show him the perfect peace and love that only He could give. More than two years passed, and I was beginning to doubt that God was listening to my prayers. I had no idea what the future would hold for our marriage.

We were having dinner one Saturday night with some wonderful friends, and they invited us to visit a small Presbyterian church near Oxford called College Hill Presbyterian Church. I really didn't want to go because I wasn't sure they would have a nursery. Chris was a year and a half old, and he would never be able to sit through an entire church service. But Gary wanted to go, so I got up early, got dressed, and then fed and dressed Chris. We headed out, not knowing what we would find when we got there.

Our friends were waiting on the front steps and quickly showed us to the nursery. Linny, a rather large black lady who was employed by the church to take care of the babies, sat in a huge rocking chair. She jumped up and grabbed Chris out of my arms. Chris immediately started to laugh and rub Linny's chubby cheeks, so I knew he would be happy playing in the nursery and I would be able to sit back and enjoy the service.

The pastor was very young and energetic. He greeted us and welcomed us to the service. We took our places in the fourth row from the front. The service was fantastic. The room was full of Spirit-filled Christians who obviously enjoyed being together and worshiping the Lord. We sang familiar hymns and listened to wonderful solos. I changed my mind about going to a church other than my own. I also prayed silently that Gary would begin to see the true joy in the hearts of these wonderful people and would want to accept Christ as his Savior.

The time came for the final hymn to be sung, and then we would head back to our lives outside this quaint little church. The pastor stood up and said, "I really can't explain it, but I feel that God wants us to offer an invitation today. I've never offered an open invitation for people to come forward, but I want to follow God's instructions. Please bow your heads and listen as the organist plays. If you feel the voice of God calling you, please come forward."

I was surprised to hear a Presbyterian minister offering an invitation. I had always heard that they didn't do that, but it was fine with me.

We bowed our heads, and the organist began to play, "I Surrender All." As I often did, I began praying for Gary silently. After about a minute of listening to the music surrounding us in the sanctuary, I felt a movement next to me. I opened my eyes and saw Gary leaving the pew and taking the pastor's hand.

I was so overwhelmed by the obvious answer to my prayer that I had to sit down. I had been praying for Gary for more than two years. Now God had answered my prayer. Before the hymn was over, another man escorted Gary out of the sanctuary, and I felt very alone. I wanted to talk with him and share the joy I had prayed for. But I couldn't move!

When the music stopped, the pastor prayed a beautiful benediction that included a prayer for Gary. By this time, I had tears streaming down my cheeks as church members came to me and hugged my neck. They were offering their prayers for Gary in his search for truth. Finally, the pastor came and took my hand and led me to Gary.

Gary was smiling and happy. We talked all the way home about his decision, and he openly admitted that he felt different. He no longer wanted to get angry, have a beer, or even smoke. He asked how I felt about attending College Hill as our family church. I must admit that the request tugged at my heart strings, but he wanted us to attend as a family and raise Chris in a Christian home. I was thrilled that God had opened Gary's heart and Gary had accepted Him as his Lord and Savior.

Once again, God had answered a prayer in such an obvious and grand way. He had forgiven me for not seeking His will for our marriage and allowed our marriage to be stronger through His love. Our life changed immediately.

The change was so dramatic in our marriage and in our lives! Only God almighty can change hearts and repair lives like He did ours. Gary was a new person in Christ. We loved attending College Hill as a family. We loved seeing our son grow up in the Lord surrounded by Christian friends who loved him just as much as we did. All three of us thrived in our walk with God at this little country church that was obviously there to meet our needs. Gary was soon elected as an elder of the church. He flourished in the position of Christian leadership—not only in the church but also in our family.

I had heard about people totally changing their lifestyle once they accepted the Lord, but I had never personally witnessed it firsthand. I had accepted Christ when I was thirteen years old. I had never been a bad person or had major problems. I was raised in the church and in a Christian home. I felt the tug of God on my heart and wanted to let Him in. I wanted God to control my life and guide me through all of my decisions, so my life didn't make those dramatic changes I had heard about.

But Gary was different. After his short walk down that aisle at College Hill Presbyterian Church, he was a new person. He was still as courteous and fun as he had always been, but now he radiated happiness and acceptance. His temper became almost nonexistent. He became the most wonderful husband and father in the whole world. God is so good!

I knew that my prayer had been answered in a real and vivid way. Our friends noticed the difference, our family noticed the difference, and our life seemed perfect. I was awed that such a big change could happen so quickly and that our new lives were perfect. Little did I know at that time that God had so much more in store for me. He was only beginning to answer my prayers and work in the lives of others around me. I would have never dreamed that my future could contain so many miracles!

# CHAPTER 3

# A DAREDEVIL IS BORN

Chris was the first grandchild on both sides of our family. Needless to say, he could have easily been spoiled and hard to live with. He was the center of our lives and gave us so much joy. My dad even named his fishing boat after Chris, who had curly auburn hair, a smiling, round little face, and a personality that would steal the hearts of all who met him.

As a small child, he was always mischievous and inquisitive. He regularly took things apart to see how they worked. One afternoon I walked into the den and discovered Chris sitting on the floor playing with some pieces of paper. He was throwing the pieces into the air and trying to catch as many as he could. He was obviously having the time of his life.

However, the time had come for a nap so he could get "powered up" for a trip to Grandma's house for supper. I carried him into his bedroom and laid him down with his favorite stuffed animal. In less than three minutes, he was sleeping soundly and in a dreamland of his own.

I went back into the den to clean up the mess he had made all over the floor. I swept up all the small pieces of paper and threw them away and then moved to the other side of the room. The folder that the University of Mississippi uses for its college diplomas was lying on the floor. My first thought was, *I'm sure glad he didn't tear up my folder.* Then I opened the folder to once again view the result of years of classes, and it was empty. Suddenly, the overwhelming realization hit me that Chris had destroyed my college diploma in a matter of seconds. He had taken it out of the folder and torn it into about a hundred pieces. All of that hard work had just vanished in the hands of a two-year-old! Within a month, I received a brand-new copy of my diploma in the mail. This time I framed it and hung it high on the wall so Chris couldn't reach it.

Chris became a regular at the Oxford-Lafayette County Hospital emergency room. In fact, after a few visits, the receptionist asked if we wanted her to post our insurance information on the wall to make our visits easier. Chris's daring little personality often got him into situations he didn't anticipate.

I was washing dishes one night, and Chris, age eighteen months, was sitting at my feet playing on the floor. All of a sudden, I heard his screams like sirens going off in the kitchen. His little face had green powder all over it. He had picked up a can of Comet Cleaner our maid had left under the sink and poured it into his eyes, nose, and mouth. He was struggling to breathe, clawing at his eyes, and obviously in excruciating pain.

Gary immediately grabbed Chris and put his face under running water to rinse the Comet from his eyes. My job was to hold his arms and feet. Then we were off to the emergency room. The doctor got Chris fixed up and sent us home with eye drops, nose spray, and throat spray. In a few days, Chris was as good as new and had no adverse effects from the burns he experienced from the Comet. But the situation could have turned out so differently had God not been watching over our son. We said prayers of thanks and praise for God's protection.

Chris soon grew old enough to learn how to ride a tricycle. He loved to ride in the driveway while I worked in the flower beds, but I had to watch him closely. He was a real daredevil and would often try to ride down the rather steep hill to his grandparents' house.

One afternoon he was riding on the driveway, making roaring noises like a truck, and laughing loudly. I had swept the front walk and pulled some weeds out of the yard when I heard him cheering and laughing just before he went sailing over an eight-foot drop off into our next-door neighbor's front yard. I was mortified and couldn't move. Everything seemed to be moving in slow motion. I ran as fast as I could and tried to catch the tricycle before the long fall, but Chris was moving too fast. All I could do was pray he was all right.

Our neighbor happened to be standing in her front yard and watched the whole thing happen. Mrs. Roulette was pale as a ghost, and her mouth was wide open. When I got down the hill to her yard, Chris was standing up staring at his tricycle. The handlebars were bent together, and the front wheel was sideways. The tricycle was totaled, but to my amazement, Chris didn't have a scratch on him. He was crying but not from injury; it was because his tricycle was gone!

All Mrs. Roulette could say was, "Carolyn, he looked like he was floating. His tricycle crashed to the ground, but he just floated." I knew exactly what had happened. God had slowly lowered my child and protected him from harm. God had answered my prayer for Chris's protection and shown His love for my active three-year-old.

Chris received a new tricycle, and he loved it and stayed on it constantly, riding up and down the sidewalk in front of our house. We would take walks together, and he would pedal along on his tricycle, enjoying being able to control it with his feet and hands. He would often make noises like a motorcycle and imagine he was riding in a big race. As time went on, he grew big enough that his tricycle was not large enough for the long legs of a four-year-old to pedal without banging against the bottom of the handlebars. He wanted to ride the tricycle less and less. We were experiencing the passing of another stage in his life.

Christmas was coming, so Gary and I decided that we needed to get a riding toy for Chris to replace his beloved tricycle. He wasn't quite big enough for a bicycle, even one with training wheels. In truth, he really was big enough, but his mother just wasn't ready for him to have a two-wheel bicycle.

We went shopping at Wal-Mart and found just the perfect machine for Chris. The original Big Wheel was a type of tricycle that was made of red, blue, and yellow plastic with an oversized front wheel and a seat that was very low to the ground. We were told that the Big Wheel was a much safer toy than a tricycle or bicycle, so with Chris's history, this was the perfect present.

Late on Christmas Eve, after Chris was sound asleep, Gary put the Big Wheel together, and I made a huge bow for the handlebars. We placed it under the Christmas tree and couldn't wait for Chris to wake up the next morning. His Santa clock went off at about 5:30 a.m. He ran into our bedroom, already breathless with excitement, and jumped on the bed. He could hardly wait to run into the den to see what Santa Claus had brought.

We slowly opened the door to the den, and when Chris saw the Big Wheel, he screamed and cheered with joy. He wanted to ride it "now!" We asked him about his other presents, and he said, "I'll open them later!" So we all went out the front door, and Chris began a new chapter in his life with a much more impressive tricycle.

He would have spent every waking minute on the Big Wheel if we had let him. He became brave enough to ride the Big Wheel down our front walk and then bounce his way down the steps to the city sidewalk. Big Wheel had a noise-making clacker on the back wheels, so Chris was always within hearing range. We could hear him rolling down the walk and then banging down the steps. This was always accompanied by roars of laughter that never ceased.

We lived at the top of a hill with a city sidewalk in front that led down to my parents' house. Chris would ride his Big Wheel down to Grandma and Granddaddy's house every day for a visit and then push it back up the hill. One afternoon, Chris asked if he could make his daily trip down to Grandma's house, and of course, I said yes. We regularly attached a small timer to his belt to be sure his visits were not too long. He knew that when the timer buzzed, it was time to come home.

I hadn't noticed that Chris was barefoot, and he regularly used the rubber soles on his shoes as a brake. He left, and within two minutes I heard screams and cries for help. He had forgotten that you can't stop a Big Wheel with your bare feet while going one hundred mph. You guessed it! He had put both feet down on the concrete sidewalk and tried to stop without his shoes.

By the time I got down the hill, I could see blood everywhere beneath his feet. He was screaming, crying, and feeling totally panicked. Well, we loaded up and once again visited the emergency room. After cleaning the dirt and grit out of the wounds on the bottom of Chris's feet, the doctor wrapped both feet in bandages to his ankles. Chris didn't even ask to ride his Big Wheel for more than a week. All he could do was watch television while the soles of his feet healed.

Chris was a full-time job for God. Our house was kid-proof. The locks on the doors were dead bolts, and all precautions had been made to keep Chris from harm. But even though Chris was quite busy and accident prone, Gary and I decided that we would like to add one more to our family. We dreamed of having a little girl who would be prissy and wear bows in her hair. We could just picture how protective Chris would be of his little sister.

Well, before long, I found out that I was pregnant. We were so excited and began the long nine-month wait for our next little bundle of joy. Nina, my mother's best friend, was the editor of our local newspaper, *The Oxford Eagle.* She included an article each week in the paper called "Nina's Notebook." Everyone in town could hardly wait to get the paper to find out what was happening around town, which would always be included in Nina's column. When I was only about two months along, Nina printed that the mayor and his wife (my dad was mayor of Oxford) would soon be hearing the pitter-patter of little feet from their second grandchild and that Carolyn and Gary were expecting their second child in several months.

After the article came out, I received congratulations and hugs of joy from friends and neighbors everywhere I went. The whole town knew that our baby was on the way. I was so excited and began buying maternity clothes so I would have them ready for the day when my regular clothes would no longer fit. I hung them carefully in my closet next to my regular clothes.

About three weeks before Christmas, we received a small package from Gary's grandmother in Montana. She sent us a check and a small stuffed clown "for the new baby" for Christmas. I proudly placed the clown on the chest to await the new baby's arrival.

Life seemed so perfect until late one December afternoon when I felt my stomach cramping and began to bleed. I prayed that God would stop this and allow our baby to be born healthy and happy, but the cramping only got worse. Then I came to a crashing realization: I was miscarrying our precious baby, and I couldn't do anything about it.

I was devastated. I had never studied the stages of grief, but I was roaring through them like a freight train. Immediately, I was angry with God for not listening to my prayers. I was angry with my family and friends for saying, "I'm sorry!" I was cratered every time I left the house and someone would ask me when my baby was due, not knowing that the baby was now living with our almighty God. I knew they were embarrassed too when they received my reply: "Oh, we lost our baby."

I knew that all the visits, prayers, and food were meant to make me feel better. I knew our family and friends loved us, but Gary and I felt very alone and betrayed by God. Our minister came to our house to pray with us and check on me. He said all the right things, but they were not things I wanted to hear. After he left, I went to our bedroom and began to throw maternity clothes all over the bedroom. I even threw the precious little clown that Gary's grandmother had sent in the garbage.

Even though the bedroom was a mess, it was very therapeutic to express the anger I felt. Gary and I were actually able to laugh about the mess and cleaned up the room together.

Additional healing came when one of my friends, Marybeth, called and asked if I wanted to attend the Christmas party the women of the church were having that day. I immediately said no. She had experienced a miscarriage herself and knew that staying in the house was not going to help me recover so she said, "Be ready. I will pick you up at 1:30 this afternoon."

I was mad again because I didn't want to go. She picked me up, and I hardly said a word to her. However, when we arrived at the party, I was surrounded by sweet, loving friends who didn't care if I cried. They were there to smooth over my wounds with love and hope.

Gary and I prayed and prayed to seek God's guidance about having another child. We didn't want Chris to be an only child, but if that was God's will, we would abide by it.

Then, after about eight months, I found out I was pregnant again. This time we prayed that God would protect my pregnancy. We also asked Nina not to share this information in her article, just in case.

My pregnancy was perfect! I felt well and passed the stage of worry. I sported new maternity clothes and proudly showed that our family was about to add one more. I loved the courtesy shown by gentlemen when they insisted on opening doors for me or giving me their seat. I could feel God's care and love, and I just knew everything would be all right.

We were still attending College Hill Presbyterian Church, and the congregation was thrilled about our new baby. They held a baby shower for me, as did a very close friend of mine. I had the nursery all fixed up and was ready for our new arrival. In fact, we had even added another bedroom to our house during my pregnancy so we could accommodate our new family member.

One Sunday when I was about seven and a half months along, I slipped out of Sunday school to use the restroom. At this stage of pregnancy, that happens often, and I found that I could slip back into Sunday school without too much commotion when the job was finished. When I got into the restroom, Marybeth, my good friend who had taken me to the Christmas party after my miscarriage, was washing her hands. We talked for a minute, and then I went into one of the tiny stalls.

Over the course of the morning, I had noticed a little cramp every once in a while, but it wasn't bad, so I thought it was just muscles twitching or the baby kicking. But when I sat down on the toilet, I began to bleed, enough that I had recurring thoughts about the miscarriage—only it was too late to miscarry now. This was a baby I could feel moving inside my tummy. This child had fingers and toes and was due to arrive in just over a month. I began to cry, which alarmed Marybeth. I unlocked the stall door so she could give me counsel about what I should do.

She ran to get Gary and told me not to move. When Gary got there, we immediately left church and headed to see the doctor. The church members were alerted about what had happened, and they all began to pray for the baby and for me. I was placed on bed rest for the remaining weeks of my pregnancy, which were long and boring, but I was glad to give this time so our baby could grow big enough to be delivered without complications.

On March 20, 1977, our prayers and the prayers of our friends were answered. Timothy Andrew Carter was born and weighed nine pounds, nine ounces. He was a chubby, healthy baby and showed no signs of having given us a scare at all. We thanked God for this safe delivery and praised Him for allowing us to have this second precious child. After just one look into Tim's tiny face, we knew he was the second joy of our life. Tim was born at 7:30 on a Sunday morning, which I really think was an indication that he was God's gift to us.

Our minister, Tom, came and sat with Gary during the early-morning hours of labor. After Tim was born and I was rolled out into the hallway, Gary and Tom were standing there and waiting with smiles that showed their joy. Tom couldn't wait to get to church that morning to thank the faithful church members for their loyal prayers that had resulted in this beautiful baby.

Chris was three months shy of five years old when Tim was born, and he was a terrific helper. He wanted to feed Tim and hold him, and he regularly brought me diapers and supplies when Tim needed changing.

I was really nervous about the baby's schedule once we got home from the hospital. When Chris was a baby, he was up five and six times every night, so I assumed all babies did that. As a first-time mom, I would run into his room to pick him up whenever I heard a whimper. Little did I know that I was spoiling him and setting a routine of him wanting to eat or play every few hours. Now that Tim was born, I began to worry about being up at night while also taking care of two children during the day and having to work. I could see myself in the future with bags under my eyes and sleeping while standing up.

The first three nights that we were home with Tim, he only woke up twice during the night. I was pleased but knew it wouldn't last. Then on the fourth night, he slept all night! I had put him in bed at 10:00 p.m. after his bottle. When I woke up and the clock said 6:30 a.m., I was sure something was wrong. I ran into his bedroom and grabbed him out of bed. Of course, this startled him awake, and he cried for thirty minutes. What a blessing! I was thrilled at the prospect that the entire Carter family would get peaceful, restful sleep every night.

# CHAPTER 4

# DAREDEVILS ONLY GROW OLDER

We actually went for almost a year without a visit to the emergency room. Of course, we had the normal ailments that needed the doctor's attention, but those could be handled in the doctor's office. Chris had thrown a basketball through the window in his bedroom but was not injured. He also had ridden his tricycle into the glass front door and broken the glass into a thousand pieces but again was not injured. God's guardian angels continued to work overtime!

Then Dave, an employee at our jewelry store, got a new motorcycle. He was so proud of it and wanted us to see it, so he came to our house after work one evening and pulled up in the driveway. Of course, we heard his arrival and went outside to see his new treasure. When we were not watching, Chris ran up to the motorcycle and grabbed the tailpipe with both hands. The heat from the metal burned into his skin and caused immediate blisters and burns. He was screaming and crying.

Gary grabbed him and put him in the car, and once again, we were off to the emergency room. The doctor treated the burns and wrapped Chris's right hand in bandages to his wrists and just the palm of his left hand. Chris spent several miserable days without the use of his hands. We had to feed him, dress him, open doors for him, and even change the channel on the TV for him. Once again, his injuries were not permanent, and we praised God for His protection.

I was an active alumna for my sorority at Ole Miss and had been elected as the house's corporation president to oversee the operation of the sorority house. During the summer, the local alumnae would meet at the sorority house to supervise renovations that were taking place while the girls were gone. On one sunny afternoon, I met several other alums at the house to make plans for summer renovations. Chris begged to come with me, and I was glad to take him along. While we met in the dining room, Chris played with some other children in the front yard. Their laughter and cheers could be heard from inside the sorority house. I assumed that laughter meant that they were playing happily and I didn't need to worry.

Then their laughter abruptly stopped, and we heard screaming and crying from the front yard. We all looked up just in time to see Chris running through the front door with blood dripping down his face, into his eyes, and all over his mouth. He was so bloody that I couldn't tell where his injury was. I was terrified he had damaged his eyes. One lady ran and got some towels while another ran and got ice. We cleaned his face off as best we could and found a cut more than an inch long between his eyes. He had been playing near an iron gate and had been hit in the face by the lock. The gash was deep enough that I could see bone, so I knew I needed to get him to the hospital. I took hold of Chris, and the two of us left. We got to the emergency room within minutes. Chris had to have five stitches, but otherwise he was fine. Again, we thanked God that the injuries were not serious and only required stitches.

By the age of eight, Chris had developed a real love for his bicycle. It was his way of getting where he wanted to go, but he had to have our permission prior to any trip. Oxford was a safe place for kids to ride their bicycles, so we never hesitated to let him ride to his friends' houses or into town to the jewelry store. He was becoming quite independent and was also very responsible.

Late one afternoon, Chris was supposed to go to a friend's birthday party. The party was going to be an ice skating party in Memphis at the mall. His friend's parents were going to pick Chris up at our house at 4:30 and leave for Memphis, but at 4:15, Chris was still not home. He was out on his bicycle somewhere, and I had no idea where. I called the jewelry store, and Gary said Chris was there. I reminded him that Chris was being picked up for the party in fifteen minutes, and he needed to change clothes before leaving.

Gary told Chris to hurry home and that I would have his clothes laid out. Chris jumped on his bicycle and raced through Faulkner Alley to shorten his ride home as much as possible. The problem was he couldn't see a car coming down the intersecting alley. The car arrived at the alley's exit as Chris emerged from it. Chris hit the side of the car and was flipped over the car and onto the pavement on the other side. He had no cuts or bruises but a huge bump on his forehead the size of a goose-egg.

The driver of the car packed Chris and his crumpled bicycle into his car and brought him home. Chris was acting rather dazed, so I called Gary, and we decided this demanded a trip to the emergency room. Gary called our doctor, Dr. Gilmore, and asked if he would meet us there. Dr. Gilmore happened to be at his son's pharmacy and insisted that we come there instead of going to the ER. He told us there was no need to pay for the ER when he could check Chris over in the pharmacy's back room. Dr. Gilmore was the same doctor who once told Gary to meet him in the parking lot of our local hospital after Gary had broken out with poison ivy. When we arrived at the parking lot, Dr. Gilmore told Gary to lean over, and he gave him a shot right there in the parking lot. He was a very interesting fellow—and a great doctor!

We headed off to the pharmacy, and Dr. Gilmore was waiting for us. He checked Chris over and assured us he would be fine. He told us to keep him awake for several hours and watch for changes in his speech, vision, or responses to our demands. After several days, Chris was fine and ready to return to his normal activities. Again, we thanked God for His protection.

Chris was at an age now that he began to develop an interest in sports and other activities. He tried soccer but never really enjoyed it. He tried football but got hurt, so he didn't want to play football anymore. What about tennis? That was a game he could play with just one buddy or he could go to the court alone and hit balls off the backboard. We got a tennis racket for him and hoped he had found just the game for him. He would ride his bicycle to the tennis courts at Ole Miss, which were only about a half-mile away from our house, and would hit tennis balls off the backboard for hours. He really enjoyed this game.

One afternoon after school, he told me he wanted to go to the tennis court for a while. I told him to finish his homework before he left and then be home by six o'clock. He finished his homework and left for the court. I was cooking supper when I heard the doorbell ring. I opened the door to find a strange man holding a bloody towel under Chris's chin.

Chris had tried to adjust the net on the tennis court, and the crank didn't catch. Instead it flew back and hit him in the chin. The man, who had been playing on the court next to Chris, witnessed the accident and had graciously driven him home.

While I loaded Chris into the car for another trip to the emergency room, the kind man unloaded Chris's bicycle and left it on our porch. We left the hospital about an hour later with six brand-new stitches in Chris's chin. His front teeth had been knocked loose, so the next day we made an appointment for Chris to be examined by our family dentist. We were assured that his permanent front teeth had long enough roots to tighten back into place, but Dr. Baker told Chris that he would be on a soft diet for six weeks. Again, we praised God that the crank had not hit Chris in the face. The injuries could have been so much worse than they were.

By now I am sure you are thinking that Chris had experienced about all of the mishaps that could possibly happen to one child. Oh no! He was just ten years old, and there were lots more to come.

Chris had begged for several years to go to camp. Of course, with his history of accidents, we had put it off and dreaded the day when he would finally insist on going. A representative from Camp Alpine in northern Alabama came to town, and we were invited to his presentation. I was excited to see what Camp Alpine had to offer but also dreaded the fact that we would have to make a decision about Chris going away.

The presentation was awesome, and the camp offered so much for boys. The counselors were well trained and loved children. The activities were way beyond any we had seen offered by any other camp. When Chris saw that they had horseback riding and a rifle range, he was sold. All I could do was confess to God that I was scared to let him go.

I knew the day had come that I would have to trust God to take care of my child when he was so far away from us. We signed him up that night and started making plans for his trip. Camp Alpine was a month-long camping experience. We were given a list of clothes, shoes, and toiletries Chris would need. The boys would wash their clothes once a week, so our list was limited to a week's worth of shorts, T-shirts, and underwear. I was thrilled at the prospect that Chris would even learn how to wash his own clothes while at camp!

Two long months passed before the time actually came for our trip to Camp Alpine. Gary, Chris, and I drove to northern Alabama in sunny, warm weather and couldn't wait to tour the camp, and I especially wanted to meet the resident nurse. When we arrived, we were met immediately by Josh, a tall, college-aged young man who would be Chris's counselor for the month. He took us to their cabin, and we unloaded Chris's trunk. After Chris was all settled in the cabin, Josh took us on a tour of the camp.

We saw the Olympic-size swimming pool the boys would swim in daily. It had a long slide that was attached to the side of a mountain. The boys could slide down the slide and land on a very large rubber float at the bottom before bouncing into the water. I was a little nervous about the long slide. Chris would be going at least a hundred miles per hour before he reached the bottom, I was sure.

Then we left the pool and toured the stables. We met several of the horses that would be available for a horseback-riding class. Chris had never been on a horse before, and I could only imagine what could happen to him while he was riding a live animal. Then Josh walked us to the rifle range, and I almost packed Chris up and carried him back home. Chris had never fired a gun, so I was sure that if I left him at Camp Alpine, I would never see him alive again. I was terrified! Josh assured us that the rifle instructors were very careful and only took small groups of boys at a time. Gary kept telling me, "Everything is going to be all right." How in the world would he know that?

Our last stop was in the dining hall and recreation center. It was awesome, and I had no doubt that Chris would definitely eat well while he was at camp. We sat down with Josh, and he told us what the daily schedule would be and the responsibilities each boy would have, including making his own bed, cleaning his area of the cabin, and being on time for all activities. The boys would follow a very rigid schedule each day, and Josh would know where Chris was at all times. I felt good about that, but I was still very uneasy about the horses and rifles.

Now the time had come for us to leave Chris in the care of these strangers. We said our good-byes and waved to him from the window of the car. It was a terribly long ride back to Oxford.

Josh had told us that the boys would be responsible for writing a card each week to stay in touch with home. We received the first card from Chris within three days, telling us that he was enjoying camp and some of the activities he was enjoying the most. You guessed it: he loved horseback riding and the rifle range!

We assumed that no news was good news, so we waited for the next card, which arrived about a week later. Again it was full of news about swimming in the creek, hiking, horseback riding, and Chris's buddy getting homesick and going home. Chris couldn't understand anyone wanting to go home with all the wonderful activities at the camp.

I was feeling better with each card we received and was beginning to relax about Chris being at camp. I was about to decide we would make it through the month with no catastrophes when the third postcard came in the mail. It was very short and to the point. Chris had written, "Hi, having a great time. I wasn't allowed to ride the horses yesterday or swim. I will be able to go swimming again when I get my stitches out. Love, Chris."

I almost lost it! I screamed for Gary to read the card. I told him that he had to call the camp director immediately and find out what this meant. He tried to reassure me that if it was anything serious, the camp director would have called. I didn't feel reassured, so he called.

The director explained that Chris had been selected to raise the flag one day at the morning ceremony. He had done an excellent job until one of the metal clips holding the flag to the rope broke loose and hit Chris on the top of his head. A small area of hair had been shaved off at the top of his head, and seven stitches had secured the cut. Needless to say, I wanted to drive immediately to camp and pick him up. Instead, we were able to talk with Chris. He refused to leave, so we let him stay.

When he arrived home after a month of being at camp, we unloaded the trunk from the car. I was prepared to wash clothes and unpack his belongings, but when I opened the trunk, I was almost overwhelmed by the strong smell of mold! Apparently Chris had not washed his clothes in a month and had thrown all of his wet clothes back into the trunk. I wanted to throw everything away but finally decided to try to wash it. After several washes, the clothes were like new.

We decided to shave Chris's head to even up his hair. He looked like a miniature bald man. It raised a lot of questions while we were in public, but the over-all shave seemed to be the best solution to the problem. The nurse at Camp Alpine had removed the stitches before Chris came home, so all we had to do was check to be sure the wound continued to heal. Once again, he could have been hurt much worse, so we thanked God for watching over Chris and sending those hardworking guardian angels to take care of him.

By the age of fourteen, Chris had become an expert at mowing lawns. He mowed our lawn as part of his contribution to the family, but he mowed the lawn at the apartment complex we owned for money. He also mowed his grandparents' lawn for a little extra money.

He had learned how to set the wheel height on the lawnmower, buy the gas, and check to see when the yards needed to be mowed.

One morning before leaving for school, Chris told us that he was planning to mow the yard at the apartment complex after school. He rode the bus to and from school, so he could get home, change clothes, and go to work. Gary and I were working at the jewelry store, so we planned to arrive home at just about the same time Chris finished with his mowing project.

At around four o'clock that afternoon, the phone rang at the jewelry store, and the caller asked to speak to Gary. I was in the bridal room helping a customer with a wedding gift when Gary came running in and said Chris had been rushed to the hospital by ambulance.

With only that little bit of information, we raced to the car and literally flew to the hospital. I remember well Gary going the wrong way on a one-way street to cut the travel time. When we arrived, we were taken to Chris's side in the emergency room. The doctor was with him and explained that the ends of two of Chris's fingers had been cut off by the blades of the lawnmower. Chris's hand was submerged in a bowl of betadine, so we were unable to see the wounds, which was a good thing.

It seems that Chris had decided that he could take a shortcut and adjust the blade height without turning the mower off. When he reached under the side of the mower, the blade caught his hand and severed the ends of his middle and ring fingers.

With the blood pulsing out of his finger, he ran to a neighbor's house and pounded on the front door. No one answered. He ran back to the apartment, but no one answered the door there either. He was beginning to get weak from blood loss, but he kept running, trying to find help.

Two technicians with the Oxford Electric Department happened to be working in a bucket truck across the street and heard Chris's screams. They ran to him and made him lay down on the ground. While one tried to calm Chris, the other was calling the hospital for help. After completing the call, the second worker immediately began to look for the ends of Chris's fingers. By the time the ambulance arrived, the ends of Chris's fingers had been secured in a damp paper towel and sent to the hospital with the paramedic.

I felt like I was living in a nightmare and would wake up to see my son all normal and doing his homework at home. No such luck! The doctor explained that emergency surgery was needed to attempt to reattach his fingertips. The chances of successful surgery were doubtful, but he said he would try his best.

We paced the halls while the surgery took place. We received periodic reports from an attending nurse about the progress of the surgery and Chris's condition. She was the one who told us that the doctor was unable to attach the tips of his fingers and that the skin at the ends of his fingers was pulled and connected over the injured tips of his fingers. He had lost about half an inch of both of his fingers.

When the surgery was complete, we were allowed to go into the recovery room to see Chris. Much to our surprise, he was wide awake and talking like crazy. The surgery had been done with a local anesthetic, so he had talked with the doctor through the entire procedure. His hand was wrapped in enough gauze to look like a boxing glove. His arm was suspended in the air by a sling on a pole, and he had to keep his hand above his heart to control the bleeding. The doctor recommended that he spend one night in the hospital. He would be allowed to go home the next day.

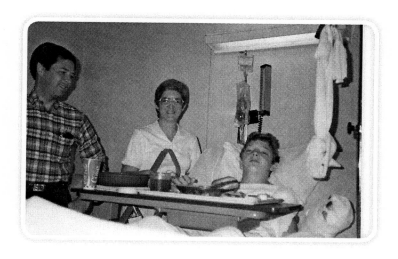

We rigged up the four-poster bed in our bedroom for Chris so his hand could remain elevated, but our active son was miserable staying in bed with his hand elevated that way. He quickly learned that he was unable to dress himself or take a shower without covering his entire arm with a garbage bag. After several days, he had gained his strength back and was ready to go back to school.

The doctor insisted Chris wear a sling that would keep his arm from dangling down. With the sling on, he was unable to carry his books at school or carry his tray in the cafeteria. He came home from school the first day, and instead of being frustrated and ready to get rid of the sling, he said he wanted to keep wearing it for a long time. When I asked him about this change, he said, "The girls at school wanted to carry my books for me, and they fought to carry my lunch tray. I like it!" All I could think was, *Thank You, God, and thank you, girls!*

For the next few weeks, Chris relished the attention and honestly dreaded the day when the bandages would come off, but his fingers healed and life returned to normal. Again, we thanked our gracious Lord for His protection and care during this traumatic time.

# CHAPTER 5

# A MARCH AROUND
# THE PARADE GROUNDS

Chris had always been a straight-A student. God had blessed him with a smart brain, and he really didn't need to study to succeed. He stayed busy with activities at school and church and working in a small hamburger place around the corner from our house. He was their delivery boy and made great tips when he delivered burgers to the students at Ole Miss. He was also full of life and laughter and had always been the joy of our lives. His goal in life was to attend Mississippi State University and become a forest ranger. We had no idea that he would not see this goal come true and that his life would take a completely different course before his graduation from high school.

During Chris's junior year in high school, we began to realize he was having problems in school. He was beginning to get into trouble, and teachers were constantly calling us for conferences. His grades were falling, and he was experiencing so much frustration at school and at home that we felt like we no longer knew our son. Chris also was becoming more aggressive, not only with us but also with his younger brother. We dismissed a lot of his behavior as typical of a teenager.

Since Chris was our oldest child, he was also our experimental child, and we felt we were learning through him.

The youth director at our church told us that Chris was having problems with his peers. He told us we needed to seek counseling for Chris to see what the down-deep problems were. I admit that we totally resented these suggestions. We thought he was telling us we were not good parents and that Chris's aggression was a reflection on his home life.

When Chris played hooky from school one day, we analyzed it as normal teenage experimentation. When he questioned his curfew, we were sure every mother and father went through this with their teenager. We felt sure his behavior would pass and someday soon we could be a normal family again.

At the end of the first semester of Chris's junior year at Oxford High School, our concern was at its peak. He resented school, church, his brother, and us. We were at a loss about how to handle this growing problem properly. We prayed for guidance and wisdom but didn't seem to hear any word from God. We were desperate for answers but were embarrassed to ask anyone to guide us. We realized that the attitudes we were seeing in our son were not normal.

When school resumed in January, both of our boys came home with their report cards from the first semester. Tim, now a sixth grader, was thrilled to give me his report card. He had achieved all As and one B. Both of the boys were in the gifted program during their school career and easily made good grades. I bragged about Tim and encouraged him to keep up the good work.

Now it was Chris's turn to hand over his report card. When I asked him about it, he very grudgingly opened his backpack and began to throw his books on the table. He found his report slips from each class on the bottom of his backpack and held them in his hand. He announced, "You are not going to like this!"

I couldn't imagine what was coming. Would it be a C or D in one of his core classes? I knew he could study a little more and bring that grade up.

I opened the grade slip for English, and it was an F. I opened the grade slip for math, and it was an F. What was going on! I calmly opened the other slips and found an F on each. Chris had made five Fs in the first semester, and our concern had just been raised to a crisis level. I asked him, "What happened?'

His response was, "I showed them!"

When I asked him who "them" was and what he had shown them, he just shut up and wouldn't talk.

Tim decided to enter the conversation and asked Chris why he had made such horrible grades. The anger in Chris's face was so intense that it burst like a huge boil that could no longer be constrained. He raced over to Tim, picked him up by his shirt, slammed him into the wall, and told him to mind his own business. Then he started to hit Tim and push him. I quickly got between the boys and told Tim to run to his grandparents' house and stay there.

As Tim ran out the door, Chris went into his bedroom and locked the door. I was in shock! How could something like this be happening to our family?

We were Christians and trusted God with everything we owned, especially our children. Why had God closed His ears and not heard our pleas for help? I immediately got on the telephone and called Gary at the jewelry store. I explained what had just happened and insisted that he come home.

Within five minutes, Gary was home and knocking on Chris's door. Chris refused to come out and shouted through the door for his father to leave him alone. Gary insisted that I leave and go to my parents' house in case Chris became violent.

I left and smiled as I entered my parent's house. I didn't want to admit to them that we had lost total control of our son and that he was arguing with his dad.

I spent time praying for Chris and for Gary. I couldn't seem to breathe or quit trembling. I was frightened about the unknown. Oh, if I only knew what was happening at our house; if I could only talk with Chris and help him understand; and if I could only see into his mind and discover the problem. The ifs were eating me up, and I pleaded with God to help our family.

Finally, after anxiously waiting for an hour, Gary called and told me Chris had left and the house was safe for Tim and me to return. We made the silent walk up the hill to our house. What had happened? Tim was excused to go to his room and begin his homework so Gary and I could talk.

Gary and I sat down at the kitchen table, and he began to tell me about the events of the past hour. Gary explained to me that he was unable to talk with Chris or to calm his anger. During their conversation, Chris ran out of the house, got in his car, and drove off.

Oh God, where did such anger come from? Why was Chris rebelling like this? Where had we gone wrong as parents? I don't think the pain of a knife blade could have been as intense as the pain of rejection from our own child and the absence of our Father God.

By this point, we were moving with robotic movements, unable to comprehend what had happened. The nightmare was getting more vivid, and I wanted to wake up. *Please, God, let me wake up and let all of this be gone!* I walked into Chris's room and was greeted by a huge hole in the wall where he had put his fist through the sheetrock. He had also thrown books, magazines, and clothes all over the room. I just stood and prayed for God's wisdom, and I had to admit I was out of human options. Our son, who had been our pride and joy, had rejected us—his family—and God. He had allowed his anger and frustration to take over.

After Chris's departure that night, we tried to make our routine chug along as usual. We had supper and watched TV for a little while. Around 9:00 p.m., Tim decided to go to bed, and Gary and I continued to sit in silence, totally unaware of what our next step should be. We decided that we would wait up and try to talk with Chris when he came in that night.

By 11:00 p.m., we were worried about where Chris might be. This was a school night, and he needed to be home in bed so he would be rested for school the next day. We got in the car and drove around to see if we could find him. No luck! At midnight, we decided to go to bed and keep an ear open for sounds of the door opening. Neither of us slept much that night.

We got up early and got Tim off to school, but there still was no sign for Chris. We dressed and left for the jewelry store by 8:30 am. We left a note on the front door for Chris asking for a phone call when he got home. We heard nothing. Gary and I both went through the process of working, but our minds were not at the store. We were devastated and gripped with fear about Chris's whereabouts. We didn't want our employees or our customers to suspect that anything was wrong. How could we possibly explain what had happened?

At about 10:00 that morning, Farrah, the mother of one of Chris's friends, called the store. "I wanted you to know that Chris has been at our house," she said. "We talked with him well into the night. It became so late that we let him spend the rest of the night with us."

Farrah said Chris had agreed to call us during the day as he left to go to school. Every time the telephone rang, we would jump to answer it. We wanted to talk with Chris. The day went on, and I left to meet Tim at home around 3:00 p.m. I always got home before the school bus came so I could have a snack ready for the boys and begin preparing supper.

I walked into Chris's room and saw signs that he might have been there. Some of his clothes seemed to have been moved. Or was it just wishful thinking? Gary came home from work around 6:00 and reported that he had not received a call from Chris. Neither had I. I called Farrah, and she said they had not seen him either. We had called the school during the day and he was there, so at least we knew he was going to class.

I continued to feel like I was in a nightmare. I felt pain every time I thought of the look on Chris's face the last time I looked into his eyes. His eyes glared with anger, and his face was tight with a look of torment. What had gone so terribly wrong that our son no longer wanted to live in our house or have a conversation with us?

Gary and I went to bed that night at 11:30, with no word from Chris. Our sleep was laced with walks through the house to check and see if

Chris had quietly come in during the night. But his room remained empty, and his car was nowhere to be seen. Once again, it was a restless night of wondering where our son was and what he was doing.

Like robots, we arose the next morning to our daily routine that was altered by Chris's absence. I woke Tim and prompted him to get ready for school. Then there was that unanswered question: "Mom, where is Chris? Are you and Dad letting him stay out all night?"

I could only reply that we didn't know where Chris was, but we were praying constantly that he would soon come home.

After we arrived at the jewelry store that morning, Sherry, the mother of another of Chris's friends, called and told us that Chris had shown up on their doorstep the night before about 10:00 p.m. Chris explained that he and his dad had an argument, so he asked if he could spend the night. Of course, they welcomed him after trying to convince him to go home and talk it out with his parents.

We were thrilled to get the call and at least know that Chris was safe. Sherry said that Chris had gotten dressed and left for school. Just as we had done the day before, we called the school and found out that Chris had arrived on time. Sherry said Chris had promised her that he would call us during the day, but at 5:30, we had not heard from him.

Gary, Tim, and I were eating supper that night when the telephone rang, and it was Sherry. She said that Chris had asked to spend the night again. Her question was, "I don't mind, but he can't live here. What do *you* want me to tell him?"

Fear once again gripped my body like a vice. I knew if I told Sherry to send him away, he would leave, and I would not know where he was. But if he was allowed to stay, he would keep using their family as a refuge.

I said one of those little thirty-second prayers that God hears in times of distress. My prayer was, "Give me the wisdom to give the right answer, Lord!"

He gave me a peace that I could never explain in human words. I told Sherry, "Tell Chris tonight that he can stay one more night, but you will not allow him to use your home as his refuge after tonight.

Tell him that at some point he needs to come home and talk things out with his parents."

Sherry agreed and said she would keep in touch.

I hung up the phone and thanked God for the words while little stress kinks were running all through my body. My mind was going wild, imagining where he might go or what he might do. I couldn't finish my meal. I excused myself to be alone in prayer.

We did get more sleep that night just knowing Chris was sleeping in a house with fine Christian people. We were amazed and thankful that the two families he had sought shelter with were both stable, Christian friends. I thanked God constantly that these mothers had kept in touch with us to settle our fears and worries about our son.

Gary and I decided that we needed to make some plans and come up with some ground rules for Chris's return. We needed to be unified, and we were going to have to hold Chris accountable. We prayed about our needs and asked for God's guidance in this critical decision. I relied on Gary's wisdom and his calm, mature, decision-making gifts. Personally I felt totally lost!

As we sat at the kitchen table after Tim left for school the next morning, waiting on God's answer, Gary held my hand and asked me to be strong. He told me that God had revealed what we needed to do for Chris. I didn't like the "be strong" comment. I knew I was getting ready to hear something that would be hard for a mother to hear. I took a deep breath and told him to share this revelation with me.

Gary said, "When we get to the jewelry store this morning, I plan to get the employees lined up and ready to run the store for the day without us. Then we will go to the Ole Miss library and research military schools."

My heart sank into my stomach, and I was totally stunned. How in the world could we send our sixteen-year-old son away? How could we think of sending him away when he was so confused and needed us the most? What would we tell our friends? How could we tell his grandparents? My mind was spinning!

Needless to say, I felt like I was going to hyperventilate, but I didn't argue. I just asked that Gary allow me to pray about this first.

I pleaded with God to give me the correct solution because I knew Gary's solution had to be wrong, but all I could hear from God was, "Listen because I have spoken."

Even though my heart was broken, I followed Gary's lead. We opened the jewelry store as usual and told our employees nothing about our problems with Chris. They were not even aware Chris had not been home for three days. In fact, no one knew about our problems but the mothers who had called us. No one we knew: not my parents, my friends, our employees, or Chris's teachers. No one! We were trying to solve this problem on our own.

We spent much of the day at the library doing research and trying to make a decision about which school would be best for Chris. We finally narrowed the search down to three and photocopied the information. Then we left for home, where we spread the information out and compared everything about the schools.

Two of the schools were so far away that we could not drive there easily. One of them was only a four-hour drive from Oxford. We looked at the class schedules, behavior expectations, housing, and staff information. We compared and compared. Finally we decided on Marion Military Institute in Marion, Alabama. The school had been established in the late 1800s and had a wonderful reputation.

In faith, Gary called the school and set up an interview for Chris on Thursday afternoon. We had faith that God would bring Chris home before Thursday and we would be able to take him to Marion. We were told to bring Chris's transcript and school information with us. Even though we were trusting God for His guidance and provision, things were definitely spinning faster than I could comprehend. I just wanted Chris to come home and be happy and content so life could be normal again. God, however, knew this was not going to happen.

Tuesday afternoon slipped by, and Tim came running through the door from school at 3:30. He was full of the usual stories about what he did during the day, what he had for lunch, and who had gotten in trouble that day. He immediately began to devour some cookies and milk and never stopped talking. He seemed so happy and so unaware of the pain and distress we were feeling. We robotically went through the motions of completing homework, eating supper, bath time, and going to bed. Tim's life was so normal in his young, unassuming way.

Gary and I stayed up until 11:00 p.m. waiting for Chris to come home. When nothing happened, we got into bed, but sleep would not come. We prayed silently for his safety and his return. Since I had told Sherry not to allow Chris to stay any longer, I was afraid of where he might be. Was he sleeping in his car? Had he found another home to go to? Was he ever coming home? The minutes seemed like hours, and the darkness of the night had a haunting effect.

I finally drifted into a fitful sleep when suddenly the telephone rang. I looked at the clock and saw it was 1:35 in the morning. Oh no! Something bad has happened to Chris, and here I was sleeping like nothing was wrong! Why hadn't I been out in the car looking for him? Why hadn't I cared enough to call around to everybody I knew? Why? Why?

I slowly picked up the receiver and said hello. There was a long silence on the other end, and then a voice softly said, "Mom."

I bolted up out of bed. "Chris, where are you? Are you all right? Are you coming home? Why did you leave?"

Finally, when I realized I was rambling, I stopped. And then there was another silence! Chris finally said in a very rebellious tone, "I am coming home, but under my conditions. If you and Dad don't let me do things my way, I will get in my car and leave again!"

Again, I silently spoke one of those urgent thirty-second prayers that let God know that I needed Him now more than I ever had. I needed guidance to bring our child home and provide the help he needed to conquer the hate and rebellion he was feeling.

Once again, God answered my prayer. I didn't like His answer, but He was the only one I felt I could truly trust at that point. Words began to pour out of my mouth—words that I didn't recognize nor would have ever said under my own strength. With a broken heart, I told Chris that we loved him dearly and that he was welcome to come home. However, the Lord had put us in charge of our home, and we could not allow Chris to come home and make the rules. I invited him to return home, and without believing the words, I said, "Chris, your dad and I have gone to bed. You have a key to the front door and know how to use it. We will not confront you tonight and will talk tomorrow. You are welcome home under our parental leadership. Good night. We love you." I slowly hung up the telephone and began to cry. Had I just run my child away from our family? Would I ever see him again?

I lay awake, praying and grieving. Fifteen minutes passed, thirty minutes passed, forty-five minutes passed. The more minutes passed, the more tortured I felt. What was Chris doing, and where was he? Finally, at 2:30, I heard the front door open and close. I wanted to get up and go into his room, but Gary reminded me of my promise to wait until the morning. I heard the door to Chris's bedroom close and knew our family was complete once more.

The next morning, I got dressed before seeing Chris. I could hear him stirring around in his room, so I knew he was awake. I hoped that he planned to go to school, but I knew I needed to talk with him before he left. He had told me during our conversation the night before that he would leave again any time he wanted to. We needed to follow his rules or he would be gone again. He had a job at a hamburger place as a delivery driver and a car, so in his eyes, he could support himself. He didn't know about our conversation with a friend just the day before.

Our friend Dede had been talking with Gary on Wednesday about finding a good car for his nephew. He wanted something reliable but not really expensive. Alan, his nephew, wasn't much older than Chris and just needed some wheels. The conversation had come back to Gary after I told him about my conversation with Chris. Gary knew we needed to remove this part of Chris's threat. Gary also knew that Chris's main aggression had been directed toward him, so he asked if I knew of a way that he could get the keys from Chris before telling him that the car had been sold. I did!

I calmly walked into Chris's room and asked if he was going to school.

"Yes," he said. I asked if he wanted any breakfast. "No," he answered. My last question was, "May I see your car keys for a minute?" He immediately handed them to me, and I walked from his room.

After taking the keys to Gary, we both walked back into Chris's room, and Gary said, "We will be glad to take you to school. We have sold your car, and it will not be here when you get home this afternoon. We must take away anything that we see as a threat to our family, and you made your car a threat."

Chris was stunned! He was beginning to see that we did mean business and that we were not going to back down just because he was making threats. We left him standing in the middle of the room with his big blue eyes and his mouth wide open! He finally gathered his books and told me he wanted to walk to school that day.

The events of the last three days had left Gary and me totally drained and feeling like we had landed in the middle of a whirlwind. We were glad that Chris had come home, but now we had the task of telling him about his appointment at Marion the next day. Just before it was time for the boys to get home from school, Gary and I left the jewelry store and headed home. We were there when Chris and Tim got off the school bus. We told Tim to go down the street and see his grandparents for a little while and we would call him later. Then we asked Chris to come and sit down with us at the kitchen table.

We had carefully laid out the literature about Marion Military Institute and wanted Chris to understand fully what was about to happen. Gary explained to Chris that we had prayed about the events that had taken place and asked Chris what he thought we should do. Of course, Chris had no real answer except, "I don't know."

Gary continued to explain to him that we loved him and wanted the best for him. The only way we felt this could happen would be for him to attend Marion and be under the leadership of retired military officers. They would show him how to be a disciplined young man and help him pull his grades up. He would begin to understand that everyone on this planet is under the authority of someone, and we cannot make up the rules as we go along.

Chris looked over the literature and was very subdued when we told him that he had an appointment there at 1:30 p.m. the next day. He spent a lot of time in his room that evening. He was obviously a little overwhelmed that he no longer had any control over his life. So many things had changed for him in twenty hours that we began to see changes in his attitude immediately. I knew God was leading us to do the right thing.

The next morning, we all got up and had breakfast. Tim went off to school. I went into Chris's room, and he had on jeans and a shirt. Knowing this would not be appropriate for our appointment, I eased over to his closet and pulled out his khaki slacks and a white shirt. Much to my amazement, he changed with no protest at all. By 7:30 a.m., we were in the car and ready for our trip. I had called the school on Wednesday and made arrangements for Chris's transcript and records to be ready for pickup on Thursday morning. We stopped by the school and then made the long, quiet drive to Marion.

Upon arrival, we were greeted by Colonel Walker. He obviously had big plans for us and for Chris. Chris was immediately whisked away, and we were led to a lounge area to talk. The colonel told us that Chris would be busy for the next two hours taking various tests that would measure his IQ and abilities. He said the school could not possibly enroll Chris now since the semester was three weeks into its session. However, they would test him and interview him and could enroll him beginning in the summer. This was not what we wanted to hear. We needed help, and we needed it now!

While Chris was testing, Colonel Walker drove us around the campus to show us classrooms, dorm rooms, the cafeteria, and recreation areas. He reviewed the rules with us and told us about the $1,500 uniform fee we would need to pay immediately. He explained the cost of the tuition, which shocked me after living in a college town all my life. The tuition was more than Ole Miss and was due in advance. My head was spinning. I knew we were where we needed to be and the money would come from somewhere, but where, I wasn't sure.

We arrived back at the lounge in about forty-five minutes and were greeted by Chris and a secretary who looked like she was a second grandmother to the students. He seemed very content to sit and talk with her, and she hugged him before she left. As she left the room, she looked at the colonel and said, "Sir, you need to see the results of his tests."

The colonel was surprised to discover that Chris had finished as soon as he did. He asked us to excuse him, and we were left alone in the lounge.

Gary and I began to question Chris about the tests that he had taken. He insisted that the tests were easy and he didn't rush through them just to make a bad grade. I was afraid he might have made a bad grade on purpose "just to show them," as he had said about report cards just the week before. He gave us examples of questions and then gave the answers. Some of the questions he provided were beyond my knowledge, but he seemed comfortable with his answers.

After about fifteen minutes, the colonel came back into the room. He eased into the big chair beside Chris and put his long arm around Chris's shoulder. "Mr. and Mrs. Carter," he said, "there is no reason why we can't enroll Chris in Marion Military Institute immediately. Your son is just points away from a genius, and his ability level exceeds most students here at Marion. I see no reason why he can't catch up with the other students in a short time."

We were stunned! Of course, we had known that Chris was a smart young man. He had been in the gifted program since the second grade and had always made straight As in school until this school year. We were so excited that God was providing the help that Chris needed.

Colonel Walker explained that we needed to have Chris back at Marion by Sunday evening. We would need to provide everything on a list that was two pages long and be sure to sew his name in all of his socks, underwear, shorts, clothes, and sheets. He would need a trunk, a sleeping bag, and towels with his name sewn in. My head was spinning so badly, I felt lost. We were escorted to the uniform shop, where Chris was fitted and would be supplied with all of his uniforms for daily wear, formal wear, and a coat for cold weather. "Oh, by the way, we need a check for $1,500 to cover this before we can fill your order," the colonel said.

When we returned to the lounge, we filled out stacks of papers and were presented with a bill for almost $5,000 for one semester's tuition. We wrote the checks and asked if they would hold them until Monday so we could have money transferred. We talked like we had the money but knew it might mean taking out a loan. Whatever it took, Gary and I were willing to do it to provide this opportunity for Chris.

Before leaving, the colonel instructed us to go to a local shoe store in downtown Marion to purchase regulation shoes for Chris. *Oh my goodness, will this ever stop?* I wondered. We hopped into the car and drove downtown. The square was so much like home, with dress shops, cafes, a hardware store, a men's clothing store, and even a small jewelry store. It reminded us so much of Oxford that we felt even better about Chris being there. We went into the store and got the shoes, which were all leather with leather soles. They were beautiful and very practical.

We gathered up the shoes, got back into the car, and headed back home. We arrived late Thursday night. We decided to go to bed and start gathering supplies in the morning. We were all tired but felt very satisfied we had made the right decision. Even Chris seemed to be looking forward to a new adventure. He had carved out a reputation for having a rebellious nature in Oxford, and he seemed ready to start over. Gary and I realized too that now we had to tell family and friends about our decision. Would they understand? Would they think we were bad parents? Yes, some actually did blame us, but we knew we were following God's will, and we felt the peace that only He can provide.

The next morning we got the two boys off to school, got the employees at the jewelry store going, and were soon at work on our own tasks. Gary shared with our employees what had transpired and explained why we would not be coming in to work until Monday. Gary called the school to break the news that Chris would be withdrawing that day. I began to call friends to share the news with them.

As I called, there was shock in their voices. There was also compassion for a heartbreaking decision we had made because we were following God's will for Chris's life. Many offered to help, so I asked them to come by our house and pick up clothes and names that could be sewn into the clothes. I asked others to label sheets, blankets, and towels. Wonderful friends would make everything happen in a very short time.

Gary and I really didn't want to take Chris away from his friends without a farewell, so we decided to have a going-away party on Saturday night. I called the church and asked our youth minister to please contact the youth group about a party. I called parents of Chris's friends and asked if their child could attend. We wanted to have a big send-off for him before he left for a new world with no friends or family.

Gary and I also began to pray about where all the money would come from that we had obligated ourselves to pay. We had written checks that were not going to be good unless we did something soon. While we were talking about our options, the telephone rang. My daddy was calling to ask if I could come down to their house immediately. I asked if something was wrong, and he replied, "I have something to talk with you about."

We had not told my parents about our decision for Chris yet and had planned that for later in the morning—but it might need to be sooner than later.

Gary and I both walked down the hill, wondering what my dad needed to talk with us about. We walked into the kitchen, and my dad had papers spread all across the table. He explained that an insurance man had knocked on the door just minutes before. The man had come to tell my dad that he had an insurance policy that had matured years before—so long ago that no one remembered it until it was found in the files.

The agent said that the policy had been taken out on my dad's life when I was a baby. At his death, the payment would be split, and half would be paid to my brother and half to me. However, if daddy wanted, the policy could be cashed in now for the cash value, and we would each receive approximately $16,500. Daddy asked me which I would prefer. I immediately began to sob. This was exactly the amount needed for Chris's tuition for three semesters and his uniforms. God had provided again. I saw tears in my dad's eyes as I explained why we needed the money so desperately. I felt the confirmation that I had longed for from both of my parents when they heard that Chris would be going away to school. I felt the peace that only God can give that came over them as we talked and planned for Chris's departure.

Friday and Saturday remain a blur in my memory. I felt like our family was in the middle of a whirlwind. We went from store to store buying military-approved sheets, towels, and clothes. Then we distributed these items our family and friends to have the labels sewn in. I went to the grocery store to buy food for the going-away party that would take place on Saturday night. None of us had time to get tired or stop running. We could do that on Monday.

By Saturday evening, Chris's trunk was packed and ready to go. We were surrounded by lots of kids and parents who had dropped by our house to give Chris a final hug and wish him well. We were thrilled with the numbers of teens who came by to see Chris one last time before he left for Marion. After the party ended and we were all exhausted, we painfully cleaned up the house and then loaded the trunk into the car.

I reminded Chris that the colonel had insisted that he cut the short tuft of hair he kept so manicured at the nape of his neck before his arrival at Marion. Chris had extremely curly hair and kept it short all over his head. It was just at the bottom of his hairline that he "expressed his individuality."

I actually like the way it looked and was sorry that he would need to remove it. He had asked me to cut it instead of going to the barber shop. Well, the only hair I had ever cut was our Lhasa's hair. The dog-grooming book had said that a Lhasa's hair was close to human hair, so I was sure I could do this. If it looked gapped and uneven, at least it would grow back and a barber could fix it. I got my scissors, and we headed out in the yard. I was a practical barber and felt that the easy way to clean up would be just to let the hair fall into the grass. I slowly trimmed and did a really good job. At least Chris couldn't see it! Our final task was complete.

We had promised Chris that he could attend First Baptist Church on Sunday morning before driving away to Marion, but when we woke up on Sunday morning, the ground was covered with a thin layer of white, powdery snow, and the snow continued to fall. Oh no! This led to more questions about our departure. Should we leave immediately to try and beat the worst of the storm? Or should we keep our promise and go to church so Chris could see his friends one last time? It seemed at this point that all the decisions were a battle. I even wondered if this could be God's way of telling us that Chris really didn't need to go to Marion at all. But God had been so faithful so far, how could we question Him now? We had a family meeting and decided to go to Sunday school only. We could easily be on the road by 10:45 and possibly avoid the worst of the storm.

The drive to Marion was long and silent. The snow prohibited us from driving faster than forty-five to fifty miles per hour. The road was slick in places, and the trees all looked as if they were frowning with their ice-burdened limbs. We were still dressed in the clothes we had worn to church, so we felt uncomfortable even without the strain of the weather. A sense of relief came as we drove through the entrance to Marion at about 4:00 that afternoon.

We were met by Colonel Walker. He escorted us to Chris's room and sought help from several cadets to unload the trunk and personal belongings we had packed for Chris. We said our goodbyes and left Chris standing in his doorway surrounded by future friends. As Colonel Walker escorted us to our car, he reminded us that the only communication that we would be allowed to have with Chris for the next two months would be written. We could write him as many times as we wanted to, but telephone calls or visits were not allowed. If there was an emergency Chris needed to know about, we were instructed to call Colonel Walker and he would relay the message to Chris. We understood the reason for this policy, but that didn't make it any easier to accept. I truly felt like I was forsaking my oldest child.

The reports that began to come from school via telephone calls from the colonel were mixed. Chris was doing an excellent job in his classes. His grades were great, and he was regularly turning in his homework and assignments. However, the stubborn, rebellious nature we had seen was beginning to show at Marion. He would try to work his way around the rules instead of following them. When he was caught, he would receive demerits. Each demerit resulted in marching a loop around the parade grounds.

I don't know how many loops around the parade grounds Chris had to march, but we got calls every two weeks that his shoes needed new soles. We made a deal with the shoe store downtown to repair his shoes and send us a bill. We also had the store deliver a new pair of shoes to Chris so he would have a spare when his shoes were being repaired. The good news was the time between repairs became longer and longer. We were beginning to see the change in Chris we had prayed for.

While Chris was attending Marion, Tim began to have problems at school. Teachers were calling for conferences, and Tim's grades were slipping a little. His teachers complained that he was lazy and didn't listen or do his class work. I also noticed that he took forever to complete his homework assignments. We were puzzled and could not resolve the problem, so we consulted a doctor, and he recommended having Tim tested by a psychologist. We made the appointment, and all three of us went together to see Dr. Marshall. Gary and I wanted desperately to help Tim before his problems became magnified.

We arrived at her office, and she greeted us with a smile. Her focus was obviously on Tim and making him feel comfortable in her presence, but she wanted to talk with us first, so we gave Tim a book and told him to read in her outer office while we talked with the doctor.

After we were finished, she wanted to talk with Tim alone. We patiently waited in the outer office, wondering all the time what Tim was saying and thinking. After about forty-five minutes, she called us all into her office together. She explained that Tim had a chemical imbalance in his brain called attention deficit disorder.

The disorder was limiting his attention span so drastically that he was unable to concentrate for more than a few minutes at a time.

Dr. Marshall recommended letting Tim have a radio on while he was doing his homework. She explained that the constant music would drown out any other distracting noises in the house Tim might want to investigate.

She also recommended getting a big bean bag chair so Tim could relax while studying. These suggestions were all foreign to the standard desk, chair, and total silence for homework, but we were willing to try. Even Tim was shocked when we insisted that the radio be on, but he responded in such a positive way that even homework became fun.

Tim was a very calm child and never a discipline problem. His teachers interpreted his inattentiveness as laziness and constantly fussed at him. Dr. Marshall suggested we talk with his teachers and help them understand the problem. She said that a simple tap on his desk as the teacher walked by would bring Tim back to attention and increase his focus on classroom activities. The disorder was so new at this time that teachers didn't readily accept the diagnosis. They argued about the findings and insisted that they knew best, so Tim was moved into classes in which the teachers would follow the doctor's findings. When Dr. Marshall's suggestions were placed into practice, Tim's grades soared, and he became an honor student.

Along with the diagnosis of Tim's ADD, we talked with Dr. Marshall about Chris. We explained that Chris was unable to remain still for more than a few seconds, and he was not even able to watch a thirty-minute TV show without tapping his fingers or feet on the floor. He was very accident prone and often would not think about the outcome of risky actions.

We also related the events leading up to his move from Oxford High School to Marion Military Institute. Dr. Marshall informed us that she felt sure there was also a chemical imbalance that causes the opposite effect of what Tim was displaying. This is called attention deficit hyperactivity disorder or ADHD. This was all so new at the time that medication was not advised. Medicine had been tested but had adverse effects that could not be predicted.

As a little child, Chris often complained that he felt like he had bugs inside his body. How we wished we had known that what Dr. Marshall was describing was a true medical condition that Chris could not control. His life and ours would have been much easier if we had understood this from the beginning. As parents, we would have been more patient with Chris, and we would have tried harder to channel his energy into positive action rather than trying to slow Chris down when he was unable to control his actions. God was teaching us a wonderful lesson through this trying time, and we just didn't know it. God saw that our experiences with the boys would help us in the future and would help us help others.

Each time Chris came home, we could see changes in his personality and his previously stubborn determination to have his way. His grades continued to improve. By the end of three semesters at Marion, he was like a new person. He graduated with honors, and he proudly walked across the stage to receive his diploma. His outstanding accomplishments had given him the self-confidence to know he could achieve success. He still had some serious bumps that were to come in his life, but he learned through each one that he was not in charge. God was!

God had answered prayers for Chris that were very obvious to us and to others. On February 28, 1998, he married the girl God had chosen just for him. Brandi has been a blessing and a gift to our family. Chris has been a loving husband and especially a loving, caring father to his two sons. He often goes to their schools and has lunch with them. They both received deer-hunting lessons and experience by the age of three. Chris is well respected in our community and is an active member of his church. Only God could have protected him through his trials, changed his heart toward his life and family, and above all, given him such a beautiful family of his own.

We have often received calls from friends and people we don't even know asking about Marion and the results we had there. Rosemary, my dear friend, gave me a copy of a book called *The Hurting Parent* after Chris left for Marion. The book helped me understand that Chris was God's child and that He had entrusted Chris to our care.

The book assured us that we were not the cause of Chris's troubles and Chris had made those decisions on his own. I began to buy copies of the book and give them to the people who called. God used Gary and me to comfort many, many other hurting parents who were at the breaking point as they were wondering how to help their child. I thank God daily for allowing me to learn to depend on Him for the correct decisions and the fulfillment of His promises in our lives and in Chris's life.

# CHAPTER 6

# MEMORIES OF A DIME STORE SPECIAL

God has a way of asking you to do things you never expect. By this time in my life, I regularly prayed about every part of my life. My prayer life had become very solid after experiences like my miscarriage, trips to the emergency room, and a rebellious child. God's answers to these prayers were always comforting, protective, and surrounded with love. I would seek God's will in everything I did and usually was not surprised by His plan for my life. I saw that I had grown in my faith so much through every experience in my life. I believed that God knew my future and revealed His plans as I needed to see them. I was very settled in my life and thought I knew exactly what would be happening a year from now, ten years from now, and even twenty years from now. But maybe not! God has a great sense of humor and loves surprises!

My parents bought our family jewelry store before I was born. My mother had worked there as a teenager beginning in 1929, so the store was a major part of her life. After she married my dad, they moved around to other cities several times, but they decided in 1944 that it was time to settle down and find a permanent home to raise their family.

My mother's roots ran deep in Lafayette County, and her relatives were many. Oxford would become home. She asked about working once more in the jewelry store and was welcomed back with open arms. In 1945, Mr. Link, the owner of the store, began to have health problems and decided to sell the store. My parents immediately offered to buy the business and became the proud owners of Elliott Jewelers.

In 1947, my parents decided they wanted a permanent home instead of the small apartment where they had lived since returning to Oxford. They chose a lot on Fillmore Avenue that had a rather large ditch running right down the middle. The dirt work would be tremendous, but they felt it was a perfect place to build their forever home. My grandfather was a contractor, and my mother had one brother who was a plumber and another brother who was an electrician. Together, the three of them built a two-story home on Fillmore Avenue that would be the new Elliott residence. Just two weeks after I was born in 1948, the house was complete and ready for occupancy.

My parents, my brother, and I moved into the new house in late August of 1948. The yard was sandy, and my brother regularly brought buckets of sand into the living room and poured the sand all over the new hardwood floor. He loved to put on his socks and with a running start, slide all the way down the hallway.

Shortly after moving into our new home, the university advertised for places to rent for student lodging. The university no longer had room on campus for all of the students who had enrolled, so local residents were encouraged to rent out rooms to students until more housing could be built on campus.

My parents moved my brother and me downstairs and rented out the three bedrooms upstairs to boys who would continue their college careers at Ole Miss. My mother would rush to pick me up in the middle of the night when I cried so the boys upstairs would not wake up. She would work to keep our toys out of the way so the boys wouldn't have to stumble over obstacles on the floor. After that year, Ole Miss had built adequate residence halls and local homes were no longer needed.

Needless to say, I grew up in the jewelry business. My elementary school was just around the corner, so I would walk to the store after school and play in the upstairs storage room or sit on the steps to finish my homework. I was allowed to walk around the square to Leslie's Drug Store for an afternoon treat or to Morgan and Lindsay's to buy chocolate-covered peanuts.

I built many fond memories in that store. My mother would allow me to pick out gifts for my friends and wrap them myself. During my afternoons after school, I would sit on the steps that led to the upstairs storage room and carve my name in the sandy old brick in the wall. I loved to watch the red sandy clay dust fall to the floor as I scraped my pencil across the surface. The building was the only business that wasn't burned during the Civil War in 1861. The bricks in the wall had been made by slave labor and assembled into thick walls between the buildings on the square. The walls were then covered with a layer of white plaster to cover the brick interior.

I also remember Mr. Bunch, our watch repairman, sitting at his bench with his magnifier attached to his glasses. He patiently worked with parts of watches that were too small to hold with human hands. He had to use the small jeweler's tools to complete his work. I still remember the day when he was repairing a customer's diamond ring and the diamond popped out of his delicate tweezers. I helped him search the floor and the shelves, but to no avail. The diamond had jumped from the bench, bounced on the floor, and dropped down through a tiny crack in the wide plank hardwood floor.

We knew that the stone was now on the dirt below the floor and could only be found by going through the narrow trap door and crawling on the dirt below. I had never been allowed to enter the trap door, and my mother had always said, "You never know what might be living below this floor." My visions were of a long-fanged, slithery creature that would eat an invader alive.

Mr. Bunch didn't seem frightened at all and made his way through the narrow door and underneath the floor that protected us from the creatures beneath. He didn't make a sound, and I was sure that we would never see him again. He stayed forever in the depth of darkness with only his flashlight and his glasses with the magnifier. After about twenty minutes, he emerged all dirty and dingy but grinning from one ear to the other. He had found the diamond and would soon deliver a skillfully repaired ring back to his customer's finger.

One of my fondest memories of the jewelry store was going with Gary to the store to pick out an engagement ring. We sat across from my mother on the small loveseat that had been chosen for our bridal customers. I had never really pictured myself sitting on the seat, but here we were. We met my mother that morning at 7:00 a.m., early enough that local people would not be walking the streets and our secret would be safe. Gary was as nervous as any young man would be, but sitting across from him was his soon-to-be mother-in-law helping to choose just the right ring for me.

Mr. Bunch was delighted to resize the ring and have it ready that afternoon so I could show it off at the sorority house during the traditional candlelight ceremony that night. My sorority sisters all stood in a large circle and sang as the candle was passed from one hand to the next. The first trip around the circle symbolized being dropped, which meant that the girl would wear her boyfriend's fraternity Greek letters on a chain around her neck. The second time around symbolized being pinned with your boyfriend's fraternity pin, and the third time around would announce to everyone in the room that you were engaged and making plans to be married.

I didn't want anyone to know it was me that night until the candle came around to me the third time. I was so excited and knew that everyone probably could read the excitement all over my face. Gary had promised me that he would slip in the front door of the sorority house after the ceremony began so he could walk into the room and place the ring on my hand. More than one hundred girls stood in the circle, along with our houseboys who had just helped serve our dinner. The candle went around once, then twice, and was coming my way for the third time. Had I counted correctly? Was this really the third time? I was sure of it. I blew the candle out, and the room burst into hugs, screams, and congratulations. We were all jumping up and down, and the room felt electric.

I searched for Gary but saw him nowhere. I couldn't imagine where he was. Maybe he got delayed at work or had a late class. Oh, well, I would get to show off my new ring tomorrow anyway. Then, just about the time I had totally given up, Pete, our head houseboy, tapped me on the shoulder and handed me a beautiful maroon velvet box. He explained that Gary was going to be late and had asked him to give this to me. I knew it was my ring!

I tore open the box to find a silver-colored ring with a stone the size of a green pea. The stone would turn different colors as you turned it and as it caught the light in just a certain way. It was an ugly dime store special. All of the girls were pushing and shoving to see the ring, and all I wanted to do was slam the box closed! They were all saying with hesitation, "Oh, that is beautiful!"

I noticed very quickly that Pete had vanished and was nowhere to be found. After about five minutes, he came in, dragging Gary by the arm. He explained that Gary was really supposed to be waiting in the hallway during the candlelight ceremony and would appear with the real ring immediately. However, Gary had been detained and had just arrived. It was all intended as a harmless joke that just got stretched out a little longer than planned. Gary spent months apologizing.

My next memory in the jewelry store was taking Gary back to choose our china, crystal, and everyday dinnerware. I could tell that this was not high on his priority list, but he smiled and agreed to accompany me. Remembering that I had grown up around china and crystal all my life, not only in the store but also at home, he allowed me to make the major suggestions. We decided on a china pattern we both liked and then placed one crystal pattern after another next to it. I realized when Gary sat down that he was growing weary of the process. I would ask, "Do you like this one?" His response became, "It's great!" Everything can't be great, but he was allowing me to make most of the choices.

After we were married, I had the pleasure of working in the store and helping young couples begin their life together with a beautiful engagement ring and all the tableware they could ever need. They would go through the process Gary and I had gone through in choosing their patterns, and some would debate to the point that I was sure the marriage would never take place. As the years passed, I especially enjoyed this process of planning for the future with my sons and their future wives.

It was a cycle of life that I had experienced with my mother, and now I was sharing this time with them. I knew these were my son's brides and that I would soon be their mother-in-law, so I tried to keep my opinions to myself. Only when asked did I comment on the style or durability of a pattern. The memories were such a blessing.

I still remember Tim's junior high school gifted teacher calling to tell me that Tim was the only child she had ever taught who knew that a place spoon was used for soup or dessert. She had tried her best by challenging him with a salt spoon and a salt cellar but had not succeeded. He knew about those too. He had developed an interest in learning about the store, and I made sure he learned it all. He usually shrugged his shoulders and asked, "When will I ever need to know this?" Of course, a mother's reply was, "You never know." Now that knowledge was paying off in school, and he was proud.

The years passed, and we watched the boys grow up, get married, and move on with their lives. We watched as times changed, and we made changes to keep up with the times, but some of the changes weren't easy. We felt more pressure in our business with new regulations from the government about taxes, new regulations from our insurance company about the state-of-the-art alarm system we were required to have, and in hiring just the right people to staff our store. We loved our business and our customers and were very successful, but there was a constant thorn in our side that something just wasn't right. Gary and I didn't really talk about it, however, because of a lack of time. We each had our separate responsibilities in our business, and we worked hard to maintain a successful, happy business.

We each had our own day off from the store but could never be off much at the same time. We only shared brief vacations and were always on call. We tried the ultimate vacation one summer with my brother and sister-in-law, Bill and Melanie. Along with my parents, we traveled to Hilton Head for a week of playing on the beach, eating out, and totally relaxing. Our boys were young and enjoyed seeing the alligator that meandered slowly in the yard behind our condo. We loved the bright sun and the sandy beaches. We loved trying new cuisine at the German restaurant. In the first two days, we had already taken about two hundred pictures of our first long vacation.

We woke up on the third day at Hilton Head and were eating a quick breakfast together. Our plans had been laid out for the day, and we couldn't wait to get started. Melanie was cleaning up the kitchen when the telephone rang. Of course, we had no cell phones back then, so we had left the condo number with friends and the employees at the jewelry store. I had the feeling that a call from home couldn't be good news, so I answered it quickly.

Mrs. Truett, our senior employee, asked to speak to Gary. I motioned for Gary to come to the phone while asking, "How is everything going in Oxford?"

She just replied, "I need to talk with Gary." I was a little offended that she didn't think I could answer a question about the store, but I handed the phone to Gary.

He listened quietly and then asked, "What time did this happen?" He then turned a strange shade of pale. *Oh no! It doesn't sound good,* I thought. He talked for about ten minutes while I tried to calm the children and explain that we needed to be quiet while Daddy was on the phone. Bill and Melanie sensed that something was going on, so now all eyes were on Gary. We all tried to make small talk to dismiss the silence but could hardly wait to find out what all the whispering was about.

Finally Gary hung up the telephone and sat down beside me. He said that the jewelry store had just had an armed robbery, and thankfully no one was injured. We were all stunned! How could this possibly happen during our first real vacation and with nobody in the Elliott family home to take the responsibility of overseeing the police, the employees, and the business? We had to make a plan.

My dad drove Gary to the Savannah airport, and he was home within a few hours. Obviously I couldn't stay in Hilton Head. I needed to be home helping with all the paperwork and the estimates of our losses. I began to pack our clothes, and we were on the road in just over an hour. My parents had taken their own car, so they followed me all the way home during our sixteen-hour drive. After arriving home, Mamie, my parents' housekeeper, kept the children while I spent hours filling out paperwork and submitting figures to both the police and the insurance company.

The robber had stuck a handgun in the face of our youngest employee and demanded, "I'll take it." Jill thought he meant the one tray of men's diamond rings she had just placed in the diamond case at the front of the store. She immediately took the tray out of the diamond case and handed it to him.

Little did he know that she had several hundred thousand dollars' worth of diamond jewelry in a box at her feet that was still waiting to be unpacked from its nightly rest in the vault. As soon as he grabbed the tray from her, he fled through the front door while an unaware customer opened the door to let him out. Our young employee was terrified and soon quit her job at our store for fear that this could easily happen again.

The strain of an experience like this made us understand the need for added security measures. We had already been training our employees for an event just like the one that had happened. We regularly would watch an employee help a customer, and then as soon as the customer was out the door, we would ask the employee questions like, "What color was his hair? What color were his eyes? Did he have on glasses? What kind of clothes was he wearing? Did you see any distinguishing marks?"

Our employees thought it to be a fun game since we even did this with members of their own families and their close friends. We would laugh and tease about some of the characteristics.

That training paid off. Jill was able to describe the suspect so clearly during a sketch artist session that the robber was recognized by a jeweler in the neighboring town of Batesville from copies of his drawing distributed by our local police department. The jeweler called the Batesville police, but they were unsuccessful in catching him. The robber escaped to his car and sped away when he realized the jeweler had his picture posted on the cash register.

Our local police were notified, and Webster Lee Foster was apprehended on the Oxford square within hours of being spotted in Batesville. He still had the handgun in the glove compartment of his car and was arrested and held for trial. This was the biggest thing to happen in Oxford ever. The excitement increased the traffic in and out of our store tremendously. Unfortunately, people were not coming to buy; they were coming to grab details of the robbery. Eventually the excitement died down, and business was back to normal.

We made big plans to try once more the next summer to vacation in Hilton Head with Bill and Melanie. We had a blast during the two days we were there the previous summer and knew we would love a week away. This time my parents would stay home, and my mother would oversee the daily operations at the store. We set the date and confirmed with Bill and Melanie. What could go wrong?

The district attorney called about two weeks before our departure and informed us that Webster Lee's court date had been set for the very day we were scheduled to leave for Hilton Head. How many times could one guy mess up our vacation? I called Bill and explained our situation, and we laughed about our attempts to vacation in Hilton Head. This was not to be the year we would vacation there either. The trial took place, and Webster Lee was convicted and sent to prison. At least we were finished with him!

The next summer, my college roommate was killed in an auto accident in Hilton Head, so I permanently decided that Hilton Head didn't need my money or time. It only brought back memories, and I was never to visit there again.

It seemed that every year we got a security visit from our insurance company. We never seemed to have enough equipment. Each year we were required to add something that usually cost several thousand dollars. At the same time, customers seemed to be getting more demanding. We had several customers who intimidated our employees so much that we had to relieve them during a transaction. Salesmen seemed to be rude and harder to work with than usual.

The cost of merchandise was skyrocketing with the rise in gold and diamond prices. The store just wasn't the family fun place it had once been.

The economy had changed not only our business but also others around us. I truly felt like the baby bird who wanted to get out of the thorny nest and fly away. But how could I leave this business that had been passed on to us by my gracious and generous parents? I knew this couldn't happen, so I prayed for more joy in owning the store.

# CHAPTER 7

## THE THIEF, THE DRUNK, AND THE INNOCENT YOUNG LADY

Have you ever thought about how life happens and we have no control over some of the events in our lives? Every day is a blessing, but some are more of a blessing than others. I wake up in the morning with my day all planned in my mind, but sometimes I am forced to veer off course and take an unplanned path.

Three-year-old Chris loved to look at shiny things, and he loved to listen as things dropped and clattered on the floor. He would sit in my lap and look at my diamond rings and giggle as the light reflected the rays of light back into his face. He wanted to wear my necklaces but only the ones that had bright, shiny stones that sparkled in the light. He got great joy out of pushing pieces of our stainless flatware down into the air conditioner vent in the floor and hearing it bump and scrape as it fell deeper and deeper into the vent.

One Sunday morning while getting dressed for church, I noticed that my diamond cross necklace was missing from my jewelry box. I convinced myself that I had put the cross somewhere besides the jewelry box, so I began to search. I looked in every drawer in my dresser. Not there. I checked my purse. Not there either. I asked Gary if he had seen it, and he said no. When I was about ready to give up the search, Chris came walking into the room and said, "I put your sparkler in my treasure box." He walked away, and I followed in hopes we were headed for the treasure box.

Much to my surprise, he opened my closet door and crawled inside. I could hear movement but couldn't see what he was doing. He emerged with one of my shoes that I had not worn in several months, in which he had hidden the cross. He looked at me with his big blue eyes and said with a smile, "Here it is, Mommy. I was keeping it safe for you."

I was thrilled to see my cross, and I knew that Chris meant no harm, but we had a conversation about not playing with Mommy's jewelry. He just smiled and said, "Okay."

Our house, which was built in the early 1800s, had twelve-foot ceilings and stately ten-foot windows. Each bedroom had a large coal-burning fireplace with a gorgeous wooden mantel above. The fireplaces had been closed up and were dormant for years. When we moved into the house, I placed delicate pieces of needlepoint mounted on plywood over the opening of the fireplace. The colors in the needlepoint matched the drapes and bedding.

Gary and I were using one of the larger bedrooms as a den and decided that a wood-burning fireplace would be homey and provide extra warmth during the winter months. My mother's uncle, Dewey, was a brick mason and always willing to complete projects for family members. We contacted Uncle Dewey and wanted to make our dream happen right away.

With the help of two men, Uncle Dewey chipped away at the brick to open the expanse of the fireplace wider. The coal-burning fireplace only measured about eighteen inches across, so wood burning was not possible, but the opening would expand to thirty-four inches before the job was complete. We closed off the den to prevent dust and dirt from covering the other rooms in the house and more importantly, to keep three-year-old Chris from getting involved in the construction (or destruction.)

When the foundation work was complete, Uncle Dewey sent his two helpers to another job and then sought a strong young man who would mix the mortar to place between the bricks. This was not a hard job, but it required strength to carry the bucket of mortar into the house without spilling any on the hardwood floor. I was thrilled to have a job outside our home so I wouldn't spend the day worrying about the mess. Uncle Dewey had already cleaned up any spills that had occurred by the time Gary and I got home so, I decided ignorance was a good thing.

Uncle Dewey found a young black man by the name of Jerry to help with the mortar. We met Jerry on his first day at work and then left to open the jewelry store, dropping Chris off at daycare on our way.

The fireplace project took about another week, and then Uncle Dewey was finished. We were excited about the progress each night when we arrived home from work. The fireplace was just what we wanted, and now we could enjoy a warm fire while snuggled up on the sofa watching TV.

About two weeks after getting our home cleaned and straightened back up, I decided to wear my diamond cross to a wedding. Once again, I opened my jewelry box, and the cross was missing. My first thought was that Chris had gotten the cross again and was playing with it.

I went to Chris's room and asked if he had been playing with my cross again, and he answered, "No, Mommy." Chris was not a child who lied, but I was a little suspicious. I left him to play with the babysitter and returned to our bedroom. I immediately thought about his treasure boxes—my shoes in my closet—so I checked every shoe in the closet and found no cross.

Then the thought hit me like a ton of bricks. Chris must have been playing with it and dropped it down into the floor vent. I returned to his room and asked him, "Chris, were you playing with my cross and maybe it dropped down into the floor vent? I promise I will not be mad if you tell me the truth." He smiled up at me and said, "No, Mommy."

Even though he said no, I was convinced it was down in one of our vents. On Monday morning, I placed a call to the air and heat company to see if my cross was in one of our vents. Over the next two days, I asked Chris about my cross again, but every time he insisted he had not been playing with it. Wednesday came and the repairmen found nothing, but at least our vents were clean. I was perplexed over where my cross could be.

We searched and searched for about two weeks and then decided that the cross had been lost. We contacted the insurance company and were instructed to call the police and report the cross missing. Then they would give us a check. We did as requested, and I used the money to buy another cross to replace the lost one. The new one was larger and oxidized to make the filigree appear to look antique. I loved wearing my new piece of jewelry.

About a month later, while working at the jewelry store, I saw an attractive young black lady come through the front door. She was looking in the cases and obviously enjoying the opportunity to browse, so I gave her a few minutes before approaching her. Then I walked up to her and greeted her while looking into her big brown eyes.

When she asked to look at a mother's ring for her mother, my eyes slowly fell to get the rings out of the showcase—but as my eyes fell, they stopped on a beautiful diamond cross hanging around this young lady's neck. I was positive it was my cross. God had allowed me to be the one to walk up to the girl and offer to help her. If any of my employees had been there instead of me, they would never have noticed the cross hanging around her neck. Once again, God's perfect plan was working in my favor. I would soon get my beautiful cross back and enjoying wearing it again.

Gary had ordered my original cross for me, and when Vicki, one of my friends, saw it, she wanted one just like it, so Gary ordered another one for Vicki. No other jeweler in Oxford ordered from the diamond company that made the cross, and this was not Vicki standing in front of me, so I knew the young lady was wearing my cross.

I didn't want to let her know that I was suspicious, so I pulled out the mother's rings. She admired several of the rings and asked for the prices for each ring. At this point, I knew I couldn't let this young lady get away and I had to think fast, so I lied and told her that the prices for the mother's ring were in the back room and I would get them and be right back. When I got into the back room, I grabbed Gary by the arm and told him, "That lady up in front is wearing my diamond cross!"

I was shaking like a leaf, so Gary called the police. The officer told Gary to act as though nothing had happened but to keep the young lady inside the store. Two plain-clothes officers were on their way and would apprehend her once she walked out onto the sidewalk.

I walked back to the front of the store and apologized by saying that another employee must have moved the price list and placed it under the showcase. "Oh yes. Here it is. I am so sorry to keep you waiting so long," I said. I was confident I was doing a great job of covering up my nervousness even though I fumbled with the rings and stumbled over my words. She probably thought I was a nut. Two men in suits came walking through the front door and pulled their coats back just far enough for me to see their badges. I could let her go now. She decided to wait and order the ring later and turned to leave. The officers waited until she was outside on the sidewalk before grabbing her arms and placing her in the police car.

Later that day, one of the police officers came by the jewelry store to update us about the interview with the young lady. She said her boyfriend, Jerry, had bought it for $15 at a pawn shop. Gary explained to the officer that Jerry had been working inside our house, so the officer knew Jerry didn't buy the cross but stole it from my jewelry box. An all-points bulletin was placed for Jerry's whereabouts, and we waited to see if he would be caught. The police released Jerry's girlfriend when she agreed to call them if she saw Jerry. She was furious with Jerry for putting her in the awkward position of being arrested.

While all of this was taking place, I was reminded of an incident that happened while the work was being done on our fireplace. Uncle Dewey and I were talking while watching Jerry place the mortar between the bricks when Chris walked into the room. Chris spryly skipped up to me and held out my diamond cross in his little hand. He said, "Look how it sparkles."

I agreed with him and then sent him to put the cross back into my jewelry box. Without realizing what I had done, I had revealed to Jerry where my diamond cross was. I had just led a thief to one of my most-prized possessions.

Twenty-four hours passed, and there was still no sign of Jerry. We checked with the police department regularly to see if he had been apprehended. That evening, we closed the jewelry store and drove to the daycare center where Chris spent his days. He loved the ladies who kept him and looked forward to being with them each day. He raced up to Gary and held out his arms as we walked through the door. Ms. Gloria, his teacher, asked about the cross and informed us that Chris told them all about the incident. We gave her the short version and headed home to relax.

We finished our dinner, and I began the process of getting Chris ready for bed. He was gleefully splashing in the bathtub when the telephone rang. Gary answered the phone so I wouldn't need to leave Chris alone in the bathroom, and I could hear him talking but couldn't understand any of his words. I heard him hang up the telephone and then sensed him standing behind me in the bathroom. He said, "Carolyn, I need to talk with you now." I got Chris out of the water, dried him off, put his pajamas on him, and then sent him to play.

Gary seemed nervous, and I was afraid something bad had happened to a member of the family. He made me sit down on the sofa and told me that the call had been from Jerry. Now I was confused. My mind spun with questions like did he want to give the cross back or did he want us to forgive him?

Gary took my hand and said, "His exact words were, 'I know where you live, and I'm going to hurt you if you don't call the police off of me.' Then he hung up."

Gary called the police, and we were advised to lock all doors and windows and not leave the house if possible. We both went from room to room checking locks and turning on lights. I made a pallet for Chris so he could sleep in our room. Gary got his handgun out and loaded it even though the police had promised regular patrols up and down our street. We didn't get much sleep during the night and were glad to see the sun come up the next morning.

After we got up, we had breakfast, got dressed, took Chris to his daycare, and then opened the jewelry store. The police constantly walked by the front door of the store and drove around the square where our store was located. Still no sign of Jerry. At around 10:00 a.m., the telephone rang in the jewelry store, and Gary answered it. He turned pale and slammed the phone down. He ran to his office in the back of the store and was on the phone again. When I walked into his office, I heard him say, "He threatened to kill my son. Please send patrols to Chris's daycare. We will be there immediately."

I was stunned. Jerry had called the jewelry store and told Gary, "I know where your son goes to daycare, and I'm going to kill him if you don't call the police off of me."

We arrived at the daycare about three minutes later to find two police cars with lights flashing in the parking lot. The workers were all flustered and scared. The police advised us to take Chris home and keep him inside and safe. We got back in the car with Chris in his car seat and were escorted home by one of the police cars. When we got home, Gary expressed concern to the officer about the locks on our old windows and doors. They were not as secure as they should be and could easily be pried open. Instead of getting a locksmith, Gary went to the hardware store and got the longest nails he could find. He came home and nailed every window and door closed except for the front door.

Apparently news travels fast in a small town like Oxford. Our phone began to ring with offers for lodging that would be away from anyone's view. We had offers for cooked meals so I could care for Chris and not have to cook or go to the grocery store. We lived in a wonderful, caring community. One call that came happened to be our most cherished call of all.

Frank, a very tall, stout, half-black, half-Native American man, called and said he had heard what Jerry had done. We had known

Frank for many years but never knew he was Jerry's uncle. Frank had been in a little trouble himself and had spent many nights in jail. He would appear before my dad in court almost every Monday morning for being drunk. At that time, the mayor of the city also served as the city judge. My dad and Frank got to know each other really well.

Even though Frank spent time in jail for his escapades of drunkenness, he had the utmost respect for authority and for my dad. He complimented the police officers and the court for their fair treatment and equally fair judgments. His respect did not stop with them. Because he knew my dad, he was very loyal to Gary and me. He was a regular customer in our jewelry store. He came in to buy inexpensive dishes at least once a month after his wife had broken the ones they had over his head for getting drunk and being arrested again.

One afternoon, Frank was arrested for public drunkenness and was confined to the backseat of a police car. Before the officer could get Frank to the station, he was alerted that the jewelry store holdup alarm was going off and he needed to get to our store immediately. He roared, with lights and siren on, to the front of our store and raced in the front door. Gary assured him that the alarm was caused by a malfunction in the system. In any case, the officer insisted that he inspect all doors, windows, and alarm sensors to assure us that everything was all right.

Meanwhile, Frank had climbed over the seat in the patrol car and radioed the police station saying he was going into the jewelry store to backup the officer. Frank came walking in the front door just as the dispatcher radioed the officer that Frank was loose. Frank wasn't going anywhere; he just wanted to help. He cooperated with the officer, got back into the patrol car, and waited until the officer had completed his report.

Gary answered the phone at home about an hour later and heard Frank say, "Is it true what Jerry has done to you? If it is, I'll find him and take him to the law." Frank had used his one free call from the police department to call Gary. Gary assured Frank that Jerry had stolen the cross and then made threatening phone calls when he found out the police were looking for him. Frank was mad and said he would show Jerry no mercy. The police accompanied Frank on his pursuit to find his nephew. Within a few minutes, we received a call that Jerry had been apprehended and was safely behind bars.

This experience showed me that God can use the roughest of the rough to complete His plan. Frank was a huge man, with muscles bulging inside his shirt. He was more than six feet tall and strong as an ox. Even though Frank had some problems and was known as one of the meanest men in Lafayette County, he had a heart for those he respected. Only God could use a man like Frank to protect us while turning in his own nephew.

# CHAPTER 8

# HIDDEN TREASURES

In mid-July of 1998, Gary was taking his usual day off, and I was running the store. A regular, grumpy, hard-to-please customer came in and demanded to see me. She came into the store at least once a week and spent a lot of money, so we overlooked her grumpy personality and tried to make the best of her visits. We always tried to please her, but it seemed to be getting harder and harder. This time she wanted to buy a silver tray as a bridal gift. She picked out one that she liked the best and asked the price. When I told her, she responded that we were robbing our customers. She asked how a silver tray could cost so much. That helped me reach my threshold, which I had calmly held for years. I looked her in the face and very calmly told her, "It's obvious you don't enjoy shopping in our store. We would hate to lose your business, but if you would feel more comfortable shopping down the street, then we will understand."

The grumpy customer was stunned, and so were my employees. I felt a little ashamed at first, but then I experienced a great sense of relief and just smiled at her. She assured me that she didn't want to shop anywhere else and had gotten the message. She apologized and bought the tray.

When I got home from work that night, I was exhausted. That customer had taken the wind right out of my sails. I was too tired to think about supper, and I knew Gary would understand if I wanted to just fix sandwiches. He quickly realized that something was on my mind and I might need to talk about it. He sat me down and said, "What's going on? I can tell you are bothered by something." I felt sick in the pit of my stomach that I was about to destroy all of Gary's dreams about staying in the jewelry business until we retired.

I started to cry and told him to sit down too. My days in the store lately had been very trying and hard. I had felt like something was wrong, but I couldn't tell what it was. Now was the time when our days should be easy. We had a successful business, our children were grown and independent, and we had a wonderful marriage. I had prayed for a while that God would show me what He was trying to tell me. I had even explained to Him that sometimes I didn't catch small hints and He might need to bop me on the head to help me see His perfect will for my life.

Well, I felt like He had bopped me. It was clear to me that I didn't need to be in the jewelry business anymore, but how was I going to tell Gary? The store had been a part of my life since before I was born and was a family tradition. It was our livelihood, and I didn't think Gary would understand my desire to teach. I had gotten my elementary education degree from Ole Miss, but I immediately began working with my mother when the business was hit by an overnight burglary. The losses were great, she needed help, and I was the logical one to step in.

Now, after all those years in the store, my desire to teach had become strong, and I wanted to make a career change. I had even been doing some research before I shared my desire with Gary so I could reveal my plan fully and with all the facts. I had never taken the national teacher's exam because I truthfully imagined myself in the jewelry store until I retired. I found out that the exam was now called the Praxis and was given in two parts. I would not have to take any further course work, only the Praxis exam.

When I got home from the store on the night of my encounter with my grumpy Mrs. Customer, I let loose on Gary. I told him I had been praying for a long time about my work in the store. I felt like a baby bird whose mother had placed thorny branches in my nest and wanted me to fly away. I could no longer stay at the store and be content and happy. I felt that the Lord was telling me to go back to my chosen profession of teaching. I explained that the store was his to operate and I would help some, but I really wanted to be a teacher.

The look on Gary's face was one of a man who had just seen a dead man get up and walk. His eyes were big, and he had a smile surrounding his nose. His joy was obvious, but I was confused. I thought he would try to talk me out of my decision. I had heard his words rolling in my mind and was prepared for Gary to say, "Let's talk about this before making a hasty decision."

Instead, Gary said, "Wow, I have been praying for two years for you to make this decision. I felt I couldn't talk with you about it because the jewelry store has been in your family so long. Carolyn, the Lord told me a long time ago that it was time for us to do something else." Now I looked like I had just seen a dead man walking!

A calm relief was present in that room that could only be from God almighty. We rejoiced in our answered prayers. We talked about the future and our individual plans for our lives. We prayed together to thank God for His guidance and provision, praying also for His future provision. We made the decision to sell the store.

Now we faced the hard part. How would we tell my parents we were planning to sell the business that they had owned, built, and raised me to appreciate so much? We decided that we needed to make some definite plans before telling my parents. A company that specializes in going out of business sales was contacted, and we signed a contract in late July.

Our sale would begin on October 18, 1998, and would not be announced until that day. Our advisor explained that the element of surprise would increase the excitement and the "need" to purchase something from Elliott Jewelers before it was gone.

We literally sat on the news until September, making plans during that time. Then we gathered our family and told them. Needless to say, they were shocked but understood. Then we gathered our employees and told them.

As I mentioned before, I had made the decision that I wanted to pursue the possibility of teaching after the store closed. I had received my BAE in elementary education from Ole Miss but never got the opportunity to teach. It was just two months after Gary and I were married that the jewelry store was burglarized in October. My mother desperately needed help to get new merchandise in for Christmas and help managing the store during such a trying time, especially since my dad had begun to experience some health problems.

The burglar had taken every diamond, colored stone, and pearl piece of jewelry in the store. All of the watches were gone, and the big, beautiful antique safe in the back room was destroyed. There was nothing to sell with the Christmas season just weeks away. I started to work full time in the store and soon gave up my dream of being an elementary teacher.

I applied to take the Praxis and was accepted for a Saturday, October 16 testing date. My best friend, Beth, and I made plans to travel to Mississippi State University early that Saturday for the test. We didn't tell anyone we were going so the news about the store closing would still be secure. I felt like I was in another world. I was nervous about closing the store, nervous about taking the test after all those years since college, and on pins and needles trying to maintain silence.

We arrived at MSU in time for a homecoming buffet at Beth's daughter's sorority house. I couldn't eat. After lunch, Beth drove me to the building where the test would be administered. She dropped me off in front and then went to visit with her brother until I was finished.

I entered the testing room and was quizzed about having concealed notes, drinks, candy, or anything that might help me or distract someone else. I quickly sat down and put my purse under my seat. We were told to place a photo ID on our desk and leave it there until after the test. I placed my driver's license in plain view on the upper left corner of my desk.

The test was passed out. After the two-hour limit, the proctor called time and asked that our tests be closed and placed on our desks. Then the proctor came to each desk, inspecting the photo ID and the test booklet to be sure all the names and addresses matched. He picked up my booklet and license and looked at them both. He looked at me with a puzzled look on his face. I began to squirm! He quietly leaned down and said, "You might want to check your name on your test booklet."

*How silly,* I thought. *How could I get my own name wrong?* Then I discovered that I had written Carolyn in the blank for first name and Carolyn in the blank for last name instead of Carolyn Carter. My fate was sealed! If I couldn't even get my name right, how could I pass this career-determining test? I knew my chances of ever becoming a teacher were nil. When Beth picked me up, I was teary and she tried to cheer me up. Our trip back to Oxford seemed endless.

Our going-out-of-business sale started early Monday morning.

The front page of the local paper was filled with announcements that Elliott Jewelers would be closing its doors forever. Even *The*

*Clarion Ledger* in Jackson, Mississippi, and *The Northeast Mississippi Daily Journal* in Tupelo picked up the announcement, and reporters were calling for interviews. We spent long days in the store working and then stayed late giving interviews.

We had begun getting ready for the closing at the end of September. Our employees took turns working in the upstairs storage area, getting stock organized for the big day. We were selling everything, even fixtures, the engraving machine, the bow-making machine, and the crystal plates and cups we rented out for weddings. While I was upstairs one afternoon, I pulled a tall shelf unit out from the wall. Much to my surprise, I found a box about the size of a small television sealed with old brown packing tape and covered with years of dust and grime. I couldn't wait to see what was hiding inside.

My mother began working in the store in 1929, and my parents had bought the store in 1945. Gary and I took over ownership in 1978. Now it was 1998, and no one had ever known that the box was silently waiting behind that shelf to be rescued one day. I dusted off the box and then slowly tore at the dirty brown packing tape. As the flaps opened, a wealth of beautiful antique purses, coin cases, glasses, button hooks, and jeweled hairpins smiled up at me. My hands were so dirty that I felt like I was committing a crime to even imagine touching the priceless items. I hurried downstairs, carrying the box like a newborn baby, and washed my hands.

I reopened the box in a private office in the back room of the store and carefully laid each treasure on a soft towel for inspection. The purses were still labeled with small, brittle price tags, none priced over $10. The button hooks with delicately carved ivory handles were priced and ready to sell. The jeweled hairpins with their hand-carved cameos waited for just the right lady to take them home and proudly wear them. Who put those items in that box and then placed the box behind the wooden shelf? The question will eternally remain unanswered.

We kept getting more requests for interviews. Pictures of our beautiful treasures were plastered all over the front page of the *Oxford Eagle*, the *Jackson Clarion Ledger*, and the *Northeast Mississippi Daily*

*Journal.* After having the items appraised, we sold three of the hand-painted mesh purses in a silent auction. We had bids that came in from all over the country. I couldn't part with the other pieces and love the memories that come to mind when I see them displayed in my home.

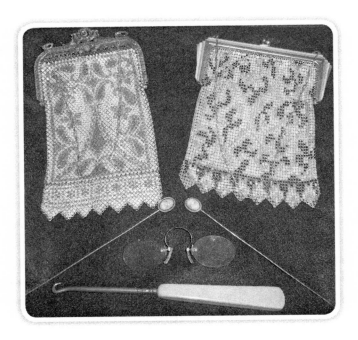

After six stressful and long weeks of our sale, we looked at empty shelves and empty display cases when we arrived for our last day. We felt a great sense of relief as we unlocked the front door for the last time. We had lots of well-wishers but not many customers that day.

On December 6, our final day in business, at about 11:00 a.m., the phone intruded on our conversations with friends. I picked up the receiver and answered, "Elliott Jewelers." Tim, our youngest son, informed me that my Praxis scores had been delivered by the mailman. He graciously offered to open the envelope and tell me the results. No way!

How could I allow my son to see what a disappointing klutz his mom was? After all, I had gotten my own name wrong on the test booklet, so how could I have passed the test? I hung up the phone and told Gary I was going home and would be back in just a little while.

As I left, I felt as though I couldn't get my breath. I had not had time to worry about the test during our sale, and I was about to discover whether God had teaching in my future or not. My future would be laid before me when that envelope was opened.

My teaching career actually began about a year after Gary and I were married. I was hired to teach kindergarten at Mother Goose, a preschool facility that cared for babies through kindergarten. I taught kindergarten in the morning and then went to the jewelry store in the afternoon. I loved the children and enjoyed my time with them. However, I never considered the developmental differences that children possess at this age that are unlike any other grade in school. Most of the children could write their names and say the ABCs, but some could not write their names and didn't even know what their last names were.

Gary and I discovered that we were expecting our first child in late September of that year. The doctor quizzed me about previous illnesses and insisted I quit teaching when he discovered that I had never had German measles, so my teaching career lasted four months. It was an eye-opening experience and clearly revealed to me that I needed to teach older children. But would that ever happen? It appeared that the jewelry business would be my career until I retired.

I drove up our driveway, and Tim was waiting for me on the front porch, teasing me by acting like he was going to open the envelope. He knew I was nervous about the results and thought it was great that his mom was sweating out the scores. As I walked up the steps, he ran, waving the envelope in the air and laughing. I finally caught him and got the envelope. I made him leave the room while I opened it. I eased the letter out of the envelope and slowly opened it. It was time again for one of my thirty-second prayers. I didn't ask God to let me pass; instead, I asked for the strength to handle the negative results I was sure were looming inside the letter.

I took a deep breath and scanned down the columns that led to the scores. *Passed!* I was ecstatic and wrapped in total disbelief. I knew God's hand had held that pencil during the test. I finally knew what God had planned for my future. I was going to be a teacher and make a difference in children's lives. Little did I know then what God really had in store for my future. Yes, I would be a teacher someday, but God had plans for me before I would ever enter a classroom. I realize more each day that it is a blessing that we can't see into our future. Only God knows what lies ahead.

# CHAPTER 9

# PIGGYBACK RIDE

Gary and I enjoyed our days after the store closed. We felt a great sense of relief on our first real weeklong vacation. We went on a cruise to the Caribbean and experienced the clear blue water of the Cayman Islands and the ruins of Cozumel. We traveled to visit with family members who lived out of town. The mornings no longer began with the buzzing of the alarm clock.

Our son Chris and his wife Brandi asked if we would be willing to keep their baby after he was born that spring. This was our first grandchild and we were thrilled to be asked to babysit. William Christopher was born on March 27, 1999. Our lives changed quickly that day and became centered around this baby. The highlight of our day was a stroll around the Oxford square to show off our families' new addition. We would take care of baby Will until he was a little older and ready to attend daycare.

Being retired was a lot of fun, but I still had plans to teach. I prepared my resume and filled out applications for both the Oxford City School District and the Lafayette County School District. After delivering those to the schools, I knew it was just a matter of time before I would get a call and be offered a teaching job.

Tim was attending Delta State University and was at school during the week. He regularly came home on the weekends, sometimes bringing his girlfriend along with him. She was in nursing school at Delta State and would work at the hospital in Oxford on weekends to gain experience. She was hoping for a job when she completed her education. The semester went well, and we enjoyed their visits. When May came, Tim moved home for the summer, and his girlfriend applied for a summer internship at Baptist Memorial Hospital in Oxford. She had been accepted and was attending an orientation meeting on May 19, 1999.

My morning had been filled with working in the yard and watering the new plants in the flowerbeds. I had some errands to run, so I quickly ran inside, took a shower, and dressed for the day. I was telling Gary good-bye when Tim's girlfriend came into the house, holding her stomach and crying. She was obviously in pain and needed to see a doctor. My errands would need to wait. Tim had just gotten out of bed and was not dressed to take her. He had on old shorts and wrinkled T-shirt, and his hair showed obvious signs of pillow-head.

The two of us headed out the door to make our way to urgent care. Tim was going to shower and meet us there. We descended the steps to the driveway, and bang! I wasn't watching where I was going and stepped on the garden hose. My ankle twisted, and I found myself lying face up on the driveway. I was embarrassed to have fallen and tried to recover quickly. I tried to stand up but realized that neither of my legs would support me. I noticed big bumps on the side of my right ankle and on the top of my left foot. My legs immediately began to turn strange colors. I was hoping for just a sprain, but I feared for worse than that.

Tim's girlfriend ran into the house to get Gary. He hurried to my side and helped me into the backseat of the car. They both got into the front seat, and he drove us both to urgent care. When he got out of our driveway, Gary drove like a speed demon, suspecting that we might die or something if we didn't get there immediately. We had driven only about a mile from our house when we were stopped at a driver's license checkpoint. Gary explained our dilemma to the policeman, and he provided a police escort all the way to urgent care.

When we arrived, Tim's girlfriend went on inside, but I was more of a challenge. I couldn't walk and would need a wheelchair to seek the treatment I needed. Gary secured a wheelchair for me, and as he rolled me through the front door, I was immediately taken back to the exam room to assess my injuries.

The doctor looked at my ankles and feet and ordered X-rays, and I was on my way to a solution. But it was not that easy! The doctor informed me that my right fibula was broken above the ankle and several tarsal bones were broken in my left foot. He also said that he could not set the broken bones and we would need to see an orthopedic doctor. They loaded me back into the wheelchair, handed us the X-rays, and sent us to see Dr. Lowe.

Gary and I were told as we left the clinic that Tim and his girlfriend had already seen the doctor and were on their way to the drug store. She had been diagnosed with a bladder infection and would see great relief from pain after beginning antibiotics.

I felt like we were playing a game of wheelchair shuffle. Gary had to put me into the car and return the wheelchair to urgent care. Meanwhile, the nurse at urgent care called Dr. Lowe's office and explained my situation to them. They had an attendant with a wheelchair waiting for me in the parking lot when we arrived. He rolled me into the office, more x-rays were taken, and Dr. Lowe confirmed the findings that Dr. Coon had explained at urgent care.

I was officially now a handicapped person who could neither stand nor walk. I was fitted into wool-lined orthopedic boots that would serve as my footwear for several weeks. I was relieved to hear that casts would not be necessary because I would not be able to stand on my feet anyway. The boots were much lighter weight and seemed less permanent.

The attendant rolled me out to the car, lifted me onto the front seat, and suggested renting a wheelchair for me, so we went from Dr. Lowe's office to the medical supply company. Gary left me in the car while he went inside to rent a wheelchair. He said that he never knew he would be asked so many questions just to get a wheelchair. The salesman asked, "How much does your wife weigh?"

Gary replied, "Beats me!"

Then the salesman asked, "How big a person is she?"

Gary held his hands out in front of him and replied, "Her butt is about this wide." That's all the salesman really needed to know, and I was the renter of a brand new wheelchair.

I couldn't help but think about how handy it was that we had closed the jewelry store when we did. It wasn't a coincidence at all. God was laying out His plan for my life, broken bones, wheelchairs, and all. I was reminded again what a blessing it was not to know what our future holds. Only God knows, and He has a perfect plan for us. If I had known my future at this point, the pressure would have been difficult to bear.

I quickly learned how dependent I was on other people when I found I could not put any pressure on my feet even for the short time it takes to get the milk off the top shelf of the refrigerator. I felt totally helpless. I couldn't cook, reach high enough to get clothes out of the closet, get a bowl out of the cabinet, or even get close enough to the sink to brush my teeth. The next week was like a crash course in how to live your life in a wheelchair.

After a week, I was a pro at maneuvering my wheelchair around the house by myself and was feeling quite independent. Our house was old. The beautiful structure was built in about 1829. The floors were hardwood, and the doors were tall and extra wide. I learned quickly how to take the turns through those big, tall doors with a speed that made my family a little nervous at times.

I also became very aware of the restrictions that a handicap puts on normal daily life. My life had become restricted to either the wheelchair or the bed. I no longer was free to pick up the puppy's toys that had been left on the floor. I could no longer access a box of cereal that sat out of reach in the cabinet in the kitchen. I had always been so independent, and I did not want to admit now that my abilities were so limited. Chris and his wife, Brandi, had asked us to take care of our newborn grandson, Will, until he was old enough to go to daycare.

We joyfully agreed, but even this joy would be removed from us in the future—a future we never imagined! But at this point in my life, God taught me quickly that I needed to accept the gracious help of others with a simple thank you.

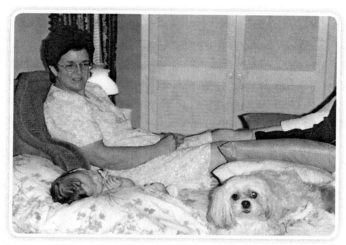

God reminded me of a blessing I had known but that always had taken for granted. He had given my family many precious friends who would become a main part of our support system for the next few months. Our doorbell was ringing constantly. I would try to answer the door but was overtaken by a family member with working legs who could move faster than I could. Standing outside our front door would be a friend holding a casserole or hot bread that had just been baked. This was truly a blessing.

Gary would admit to anyone that he has very limited skills in regular daily nutrition. His specialties are scrambled eggs and pancakes. Instead we feasted on the favorite foods of our wonderful friends and neighbors. I added a daily prayer that the food would nourish my body and strengthen the breaks in my legs but not become a problem that would require a larger wheelchair before the ordeal was over and I could exercise once more. God answered that prayer in time with healed legs and no gain in weight. Only God could have done that with all the delicious food we had.

Our house was constantly active, with friends who would come to check on me and stay for short visits. Most would come with flowers or a gift in hand that made me feel so loved. Even though I couldn't offer them something to drink by myself, I learned to wait patiently for my family to be the perfect hosts. They never let me down!

For more than twenty years, Beth Fitts and Rosemary Brewer, two precious friends, had joined me weekly for a prayer time at church and then a cup of coffee at a local restaurant, where we would share stories of our week and lots of laughter. After my accident, Beth and Rosemary insisted on continuing this tradition at my house. Gary supported the idea because he knew I was always a better person and easier to live with after my time with these friends. He insisted on making the coffee and would even use the cream pitcher instead of the milk carton that was so standard in our home.

Beth and Rosemary would arrive at my house ready to check on my progress, and then we would spend about thirty minutes praying for each other, our children, and the needs in our lives. I was always propped up in bed and eager for their arrival. Gary would place chairs near my bed for them and then place a cover over my potty chair to serve as a table for their coffee. We would pray, and then Gary would serve as the host and provide coffee and sometimes goodies that other friends had brought. These friends didn't limit their prayers for me to just that once-a-week prayer time. They prayed daily for my legs to heal and my overall health to be restored.

I still could not put any pressure on my legs, which meant I could not stand up at all. However, I had learned to do some things that gave me a sense of being normal. My arms were getting stronger from getting myself in and out of the wheelchair and into a chair or the bed. I worried about developing biceps that would become unsightly when I recovered from my untimely accident.

I discovered quickly that the one room in the house that would not allow my entrance was the master bathroom. In an earlier renovation and addition, the bathroom door had been moved from the hallway to the bedroom. Because of the location of the toilet, the door had to be slightly narrower than a standard doorway. This had never been a problem before, but it became a barrier to a handicapped person in a wheelchair.

Gary would pick me up and carry me to the toilet. Then when the job was finished, he would return to get me. He would pick me up and carry me to the shower but never without a cordless telephone that would allow me to call for help if needed. He would sit me down on the edge of the bathtub and place garbage bags over my legs, with duct tape just below my knees. This would keep the boots I wore on both legs from getting wet while I enjoyed the warm water of the shower. Of course, after a while I developed a rash just below my knees where the duct tape was placed. I still insisted that I wanted to exercise my independence by having a shower by myself and not be assisted by anyone else, rash or no rash.

One day Gary decided that my transition from the bed to the shower would be much easier if I would take off all my clothes while seated on the side of the bed so he could place the garbage bags over my legs there. Then all he would have to do was carry me into the bathroom and place me on the shower chair that was awaiting my arrival.

Even though I worried that a family member or friend might walk into the house and see me sitting naked on the side of the bed with garbage bags on my legs, I agreed. It seemed to take forever to get the job done. Getting undressed and being bagged up was a chore in itself and quite a lengthy process, but eventually, we were ready for the move.

Gary then decided that the strain on his back would be eased if he carried me piggyback. Well, I almost fell off the side of the bed laughing. He was always joking and trying to make me laugh, so I thought he was only teasing me. But he was not teasing!

After I composed myself, he backed up in front of me and told me to jump on. I put my arms around his neck and my garbage-bagged legs around his waist. He grunted when he lifted me off the bed, and we started our short journey to the bathroom, with Gary walking slowly because of the weight on his back.

When we arrived at the door to the bathroom, we suddenly realized that we could not enter walking forward. The large boots on my legs prevented us from getting through the doorway, so we had to come up with another plan.

Gary stood at the doorway with me on his back as we discussed our options. It was during this discussion that I realized that a trip to the toilet before my shower would not be a bad idea. I told Gary about my altered plan and was reminded that we first had to get into the bathroom.

We finally decided that we would try to enter the bathroom sideways. That way I could put one leg through the narrow doorway at a time and our bodies would just slide on through. We approached the doorway with Gary giving me instructions about my part in this plan and what I was supposed to do.

I did just as I was told. My left leg entered the doorway first, and then it was time for our bodies to enter in unison. The fit was a little snug, we noticed, but we could make it. Or so we thought! We got halfway in through the door and got stuck, left foot in and right foot out—naked and needing to pee! We were in trouble and could not move either way.

We worked and worked to free our bodies, but no luck! During the struggle, we both looked into the bathroom at the same time, and in the mirror on the opposite wall, we witnessed our predicament first hand. We realized just how ridiculous we looked and began to laugh, and our laughter brought on other problems. The more I laughed, the more I needed to pee. I told Gary that we had an emergency and we needed to get free as soon as possible. I even whispered a prayer that God would help us out of this untimely situation. He must have heard me, because we finally slipped through the door and were free at last.

After my trip to the toilet and a wonderful shower, Gary and I sat down to discuss the problem with getting in and out of the bathroom. The only solution was to use the bathroom on the other side of the house. The door there was wide, and the bathroom was large enough to maneuver a wheelchair, so only limited help would be needed. A path was made through the dining room with the large antique dining table and matching chairs giving up their prominence by being pushed aside. Now I would be able to roll my wheelchair all the way across the house with no obstacles in the way.

You remember the part about the house being old? Well, now the obstacle was the bathtub. Our second bathroom was graced by a beautiful, old claw-foot bathtub. The tub was tall and not easily accessed from a seated position in a wheelchair, but I was determined that this too would be conquered by the willpower to solve the problem.

In a matter of days, I learned how to undress while seated in my wheelchair, wrap garbage bags and duct tape over my own legs, and hoist myself, with my now-strong arms, up onto the side of the bathtub. I would then pick my legs up one at a time and put them into the tub. Still seated on the edge of the tub, I would grab the handle of the shower chair and lift my body into the tub. Oh, the rewards of my labor! I enjoyed long, warm showers and developed yet another stage of independence.

# CHAPTER 10

# RESTING IN GOD'S ARMS

Within the two weeks following my accident, I became independent enough to dress by myself, shower by myself, go to the bathroom by myself, and retrieve food by myself as long as it was left at an acceptable height. My family became adept at putting things on the lower shelves of the refrigerator so I could reach them easily. Cereal bowls, plates, and glasses were left out on the counter so I could reach them. The sink and the stovetop were still much too high, so I was unable to cook or wash dishes, but at least I was not quite the burden to my family that I had been in the beginning of the journey.

I was still unable to leave the house by myself because every door had a monster that stared me in the face each time I opened the door. Every exit had a step down that could only be conquered by a driver for my wheelchair. I enjoyed sitting on our front porch and talking with neighbors or just reading a book. However, once I was on the porch, I was held captive by that one step that prohibited my entrance back into the house without someone to lean my wheelchair backward and pull it into the house. I made sure that I always had a cordless telephone by my side so I could call for help when needed.

By the end of May, calls were being made by local principals for future teachers at their schools. I received a call from Mr. Herod, the principal at Lafayette Elementary, for an interview. I was so excited and readily accepted the date and time that had been scheduled for me to be interviewed and be hired for a teaching job. I never considered that my interview would be totally different from that of any other applicant. I obviously could not go alone. I would need someone to drive me to the interview and then guide my wheelchair to the building. Gary graciously agreed to help me.

My big day began several hours before my interview was to take place. I took a shower and washed my hair. I put on makeup, which was not a regular part of my routine during this time. Finally, I was ready to go. Gary loaded me and my wheelchair into the car, and off we went.

The interview was wonderful. Mr. Herod made me feel very comfortable and never gave any indication that I might not get hired because of my temporary disability. I had full faith that my breaks would heal in time to start school in July, even though Dr. Lowe, my doctor, told me that I would not be able to stand on my feet long enough to begin teaching in the fall. I felt good about the interview and confident that I would soon be teaching. Mr. Herod said that all interviews would be completed by the first week in June and told me he would give me a call.

Gary had made plans to attend the upcoming Promise Keepers Conference in Memphis on June 4-5. He put his plans out of his mind when my accident occurred because of my limitations. He had become my total support system and also kept the house straight for the many guests who came. He cooked (actually, he warmed up the wonderful delicacies that our friends brought), washed our clothes, carried me back and forth to the doctor, and literally saw to my every need. When I realized he was not considering going to the conference, I began trying harder to show him just how independent I had become. He had sacrificed so much for me following the events of May 19 that I wanted to give him a short weekend off to celebrate God's work in song and praise.

Tim had promised his dad that he would assist me and be sure that my every need was met while Gary was gone during the weekend. I had learned how to raise myself out of my wheelchair and up onto our antique, king-size bed. The mattress was high, and it was a challenge every time I wheeled myself beside it. I learned from experience that as long as someone was there to catch me if I crashed, I could conquer the bed. This would be the only time I would not be in my wheelchair while Gary was gone. I could get into one of our comfortable chairs in the den without help, so some time in front of the TV seemed like a release from prison.

Gary still didn't seem totally convinced he should leave me. He was especially concerned that I would spend so much time on Friday evening and Saturday without him by my side. He had always been just a call away if I needed anything. I assured him that I would be fine, but his hesitance remained.

During our prayer time that week, I told Beth and Rosemary about Gary's concerns. We prayed for a solution to the problem so Gary would feel he could leave me for a short time. After we prayed and the last amen was said, Beth looked at me and said, "I don't have any plans for Saturday. Would he feel better if I came and spent the day with you?"

Well, God had answered our prayers! When I told Gary that Beth was coming to spend the day, he smiled and agreed to go to the conference. I could still sense his concern, but I could see the excitement in his face just knowing that his weekend would be filled with praise to God in worship and song. I felt a sense of excitement too! I was going to prove to my family, friends, and the world just how well I was doing and how independent I had become.

With each question from Gary, I assured him that I would be fine. In the back of my mind, I felt a twinge of fear about not having him at home to assist me when needed, but I was sure everything would be fine. After all, he was only going to be gone a short time.

Well, Friday afternoon came, and he left to meet the other men who would be attending the conference with him. The house seemed so quiet. The creaks of our hardwood floors seemed louder than usual in the quiet of the late afternoon. I could feel chill bumps racing up and down my arms. The hum of the refrigerator almost sounded like the roar of a lion in the silence.

I was actually amazed that I was hearing sounds that I had never heard with others around me. I spent the time reading, watching TV, and talking with friends on the telephone. Tim prepared supper for us and graciously cleaned up the kitchen. I watched more television until it was time to go to bed. I didn't sleep at all until I heard the front door open and close. Then I knew Gary was home for the night, and I could relax.

Gary got up early Saturday morning, dressed, and left for Memphis without waking me. I woke up early on Saturday morning and got dressed and brushed my teeth. In the beauty of the morning sun, the sounds had vanished and I realized that the creatures of the night were gone. Tim left to go to work, and once again, I was at home alone.

I was so excited to hear the sweet voice of my friend coming through the front door. Beth would serve as my guardian angel for the day. With the loving concern of a true friend, she checked to see if I was hungry, thirsty, or needed anything. She helped me fix a bowl of cereal for breakfast, and we sat together in the kitchen while I ate.

When all of my needs were met, we sat in the den and talked as if we had not seen each other in months. I looked forward to our visit to catch up on the outside world that I missed so desperately. We would take breaks in the conversation to refill the seemingly bottomless coffee cups, whose emptiness yearned to be filled again with hot, steaming coffee.

The morning passed so quickly that lunch time approached much sooner than expected. Beth was going to be sure that I didn't go hungry, so she headed for the kitchen to fix lunch. When it was ready, she called me to a bountiful feast in the kitchen. We still talked all during the meal, taking a break in the conversation only for another bite of food.

After lunch, Beth washed the dishes and asked what I would like to do during the afternoon. I sat in my wheelchair and realized that I had become somewhat short of breath and a little dizzy. I thought that maybe we had talked so much that I was just winded from all the conversation.

I told Beth that I was not feeling very well, and she insisted that I go and lie down in the bed. As she finished in the kitchen, I wheeled myself to the bedroom and lifted myself up onto the tall, antique bed. As I lay down, I felt as though the entire room was spinning out of control. After a while, I began to realize that the dizziness was subsiding and my breathing was coming easier. Beth pulled up a chair next to my bed and sat quietly reading a magazine while I rested for a little while.

Gary returned in the late afternoon, refreshed and bubbling about the things that had happened during the conference. He was very inspired by the speakers and had bought some of the CDs prepared by the Promise Keepers Praise Band. Gary thanked Beth for her gracious attendance in his absence. Beth and I both could see the restoration that had taken over his spirit in the short time he had been away. She picked up her purse and headed back to her home and family.

All during supper, Gary and I talked about his conference. He described the speakers with such detail that I honestly felt as if I had been with him in the stadium seats. He described songs that had been sung and the way the men prayed for each other and shared the bond of God's love. I loved hearing about the conference and was so proud he was able to attend.

After he told me about the conference, he asked how my weekend had been. I told him about all the uneventful happenings of Friday night and then explained about the fun Beth and I had just talking and catching up. On purpose, I left out the part about not feeling well and had sworn Beth to secrecy. I assured her that I was better and Gary did not need to worry about something so minor.

On Sunday morning, Gary went to Sunday school but was home almost within the hour to care for me. He fixed lunch, and we spent an afternoon visiting with friends at our home. From time to time, I would again feel weak and short of breath during the afternoon. I didn't want to alarm anyone—Gary or the friends who came by our house—so I sat quietly and never said a word about my condition.

After supper that night, Gary told me that he wanted to do something special for me. I had always taken great care to be sure that my pedicure was perfect during sandal season, and after two and a half weeks, it was something less than perfect. My toes were visible at the ends of the wool-lined black boots that were my fashion statement at the time. I had become very conscious of that fact and often tried to hide my toes to conceal the ragged-looking toenail polish.

Gary told me that he knew I could not physically polish my own toenails, so he wanted to do the job for me. Needless to say, I was a little hesitant, knowing he had never done this before. The doctor had said that at this stage in my recovery, I could remove the boots for a short time and wash my legs and feet, but I was not to stand or put any pressure on my legs.

Well, the process began. Gary got a bowl of water and some soap. He also got the polish remover and toenail polish, along with all of the other needed supplies. He positioned me in front of the small TV in the kitchen so I could be entertained, and then he began by removing my boots. He removed the old polish and then washed my legs and feet. My legs had little cramps running up and down them, so Gary massaged my legs, which felt heavenly after being confined for so long. Wool-lined boots in the heat of a Mississippi summer do not equal comfort!

Gary then dried my feet and began the polishing process. I must admit that he did an excellent job and could have had a different career if he had chosen to. After my nails had dried, he carefully replaced the boots. I noticed that I was beginning to feel tired. The process had taken much longer than it did when I polished my own nails.

I told Gary that I was going to get ready for bed while he washed the supper dishes. I went into the bedroom and struggled to undress and put on my pajamas while sitting in my wheelchair. Then I rolled myself across the house to brush my teeth. Exhausted by this time, I rolled back to the bedroom and hoisted myself onto the bed.

My body seemed to gradually relax from my head to my toes as I stretched out, but instead of falling asleep, my body then began shifting into another dimension, and I was totally unaware of what was taking place around me. I was at total peace.

As Tim walked by our bedroom door about 10:00 that evening, I had my arm over my face, and he heard me whispering something. He came into the room. I was softly calling Gary's name and saying that I didn't feel well. After Tim retrieved Gary from his dishwashing duties, I told Gary that I didn't feel well. Gary and Tim both noticed how labored my breathing had become and that my lips were becoming blue in color. When Gary suggested I needed to go to the hospital, I told him that I wasn't sure he could get me into the car by himself. He chuckled and explained that he was going to call the ambulance. After that comment, I spoke no more.

Gary immediately called for an ambulance and then prayed while waiting for its arrival. During the short ambulance ride to the hospital, my breathing stopped, and my heart ceased its regular beat. I was allowed admittance into the loving arms of our Lord and Savior.

Since that night, I have often thought about the chaos and trauma that a baby experiences during childbirth. He has been held close for nine months, close enough to hear his mother's heartbeat, close enough to feel the soothing strokes of his mother's hand across her tummy, and close enough to hear her sweet voice as she sings to him. Then during the birth process, he is squeezed and is no longer suspended in the warm, protective fluids within his mother's womb.

For hours, he is pushed with every contraction of his once-safe and secure environment. He can hear the moans that his mother makes as she prepares for the birth of her long-awaited baby. Then the moment arrives, and he slips from the womb, through the birth canal, and into a world of bright lights, loud noises, and nurses cleaning his eyes, his ears, and his mouth. He no longer feels the safe, secure warmth of his mother's body. He is placed under bright lights while the nurse weighs him, bathes him, and dresses him in clothes. He hears a voice that sounds like that same sweet voice that sang to him, but he must wait until the procedures are finished before he is placed in his mother's waiting arms.

# CHAPTER 11

## MOM'S CALLING YOU, DAD

Subject: Urgent Prayer Request
Date: Mon, 07 Jun 1999, 10:17 a.m.
From: Gary and Carolyn Carter
To: (recipients)

Dear Friends,

Some of you will already know that my wife, Carolyn, suffered a fall two and a half weeks ago that left her with a broken right leg and a broken left foot. Last night, Sunday, she had a sudden and near-fatal complication from the injuries.

Around 10:00 p.m. she began to feel extremely bad, with labored breathing. When my son called me to her bedside, I found her cyanotic. She had a bluish coloration in her skin and lips. We knew that the oxygen level in her blood was dangerously diminished and she was in distress. We called for an ambulance, which arrived quickly and transported her the half mile to the hospital. In that short period of time, she took a very bad downturn, and upon arrival at the ER, she had no pulse or blood pressure. But for the grace of almighty God alone, she would not have been resuscitated.

The early diagnosis was a pulmonary embolism (blood clot) that had traveled from the site of the bone fracture to her lung(s). They told us that: (1) she might not pull through; (2) that she might pull through with some degree of brain injury from the twenty minutes with no vitals; or (3) that she might pull through with a full recovery.

The pulmonologist has spoken with me this morning, and the short version of his briefing is essentially positive. Most of the indicators he observed show improvement. She continues to be on a respirator and is sedated. The next twenty-four to forty-eight hours are very important, to say the least.

My family and the friends who gathered with us in the late hours last night have placed Carolyn's care in the hands of almighty God, and we are trusting Him for what He will do. Will you pray with us for her full recovery? Please lift up the medical professionals as they have ministered to her with tenderness and compassion. We voice thanks for the work they have done and the manner in which they have served her. We ask for wisdom, sensitivity, and compassion from them, and we pray that God will use the circumstances for His glory. Please pray also for Carolyn's mother and father, who are deeply shaken by this, as well as my sons, Chris and Tim.

Thank you for your care for our need.

Gary

These words went out to my email contact list and also to Carolyn's following the most-anguished night of my life. I had nearly lost my wife to an unexpected medical complication, and at this point, I wasn't sure that still wouldn't happen.

Two weeks earlier, on May 19, 1999, to be exact, Carolyn had stepped on a garden hose left on the driveway and taken a tumble that resulted in what was surely a bad sprain. After being told that she had fallen, I went out to check on her. To know Carolyn is to know what a positive and resilient person she is, so when I stepped out onto the porch, instead of finding her lying on the concrete and moaning, I found her *standing* beside the car, bracing against the already open door, blushing, and laughing at her clumsiness. After Carolyn sat down on the car seat, we examined her leg and determined she must have suffered a bad sprain. The pain was increasing, as was the swelling and discoloration, so I easily persuaded her to let me take her to the urgent care facility a short drive away.

Small towns are great! Everybody knows everybody, which can be a very comforting thing. Dr. David Coon, a friend we have seen many times with all of the usual afflictions, emerged from the examination room with something of a grin to blunt the "this-isn't-what-you-are-wanting-to-hear" report and told me that it looked like we were dealing with something more than a sprain.

During his examination, Carolyn had told him of additional pain in her left foot, so he X-rayed both sites of pain. The X-rays revealed Carolyn's sprain was in reality a minor fracture in her right fibula (small leg bone) just above the ankle and also a break in one of the small bones of her left foot. He showed me the X-rays and advised us that he would call the orthopedist to let him know we were on the way. He had taken care of us but needed to refer us to a specialist.

We met orthopedist and friend Dr. Ernie Lowe at his office a couple of blocks away from urgent care and got the relatively good news that due to the nature of the breaks, and because the ends of the leg fracture were not displaced, Carolyn would not require surgery, but no weight could be placed on the leg or displacement could result.

*No problem,* we thought, but with both the right leg and the left foot broken, how would we manage? There was no other way but that Carolyn would have to get along in a wheelchair. By avoiding surgery, we both felt like we had dodged a bullet, and so with an air splint on the broken foot and an orthopedic boot on the broken leg, a wheelchair was the answer.

The house we had lived in for twenty-nine years was an old one, which was both a plus and a minus. On the plus side, the doors were wider than normal, which made it easier for Carolyn to wheel around; the minus side was that no entrance to the house had less than four steps to negotiate. The Carters were getting an eye-opening look at the realities of disability. In fact, only days after the accident, we had commented that instead of asking, "God, why did you let this happen?" we should have asked, "God, what do you want us to learn from this?"

We now considered the distinct possibility that God was showing us in a temporary circumstance what is for others a permanent lifestyle. It was sobering. It was also good that at the time we had no idea how seriously we had underestimated the lesson we would soon face.

We managed rather well for the next couple of weeks. Carolyn's parents and Chris, Brandi, and Tim, my sons and daughter-in-law, pitched in however they might, and friends prepared and delivered so many husband-helper meals to freeze and heat later that I began to realize just how widely it was known that I was no cook. My longstanding deal with Carolyn had always been, "You cook; I'll clean up."

A Promise Keepers conference was scheduled in nearby Memphis on June 4-5, and for some time I had planned to attend with friends from Oxford. It would be held Friday night and Saturday until mid-afternoon. As we talked about whether I still should attend, Carolyn was very supportive of the idea since I would come home Friday night and be back home again by mid-afternoon Saturday. On top of that, our younger son, Tim, was at home for the summer, and Carolyn's friend, Beth, had offered to spend the day with Carolyn on Saturday, so it was agreed that I should go.

The conference was refreshing, but it was good to get back home. Carolyn did fine, though she said she wasn't feeling as well as she had been. The next day, Sunday, she said she didn't really feel bad, but she didn't feel ready to dress and go to church, so she stayed in. We just took it easy that afternoon and enjoyed a brief visit by another couple.

It wasn't until sometime later that I thought very much about her not feeling well.

Sunday night was a little weird. To lift her spirits, I prepared supper—husband helper. After supper, I left the dishes on the island in the kitchen to be dealt with later and told Carolyn to position her wheelchair so she could watch TV while I sat on the floor in front of her to give her a pedicure. That's something I'd never done before, but Carolyn had last polished her toenails the night before her accident and by now the polish was starting to grow off in the back. A pedicure would be a boost to her spirits, or at least I hoped so.

She enjoyed the pedicure, but it took forever, and when I was finished, I suggested she roll in and get ready for bed while I finished cleaning up the kitchen. By now it was close to 10:00. I put her orthopedic appliances back on and sent her off. About ten minutes later, Tim came to the kitchen and said, "Dad, Mom wants you. She says she's not feeling good." Even today those words cause an uneasy stirring deep inside me.

I left the dishes and went to the bedroom to find Carolyn on the bed with her forearm across her forehead. Her color wasn't quite right.

"How are you doing?" I asked.

"Not too good," was her weak reply.

"Tell me about it," I pressed for more detail.

"I just don't feel good."

I began to ask yes or no questions. "Are you hurting anywhere?"

"No."

"How about in your chest, any pressure?"

"No."

"Do you have any numbness or tingling anywhere, like your neck or arm?"

"No."

Each response was woozier than the one before. I could tell she was sinking, but I had no idea how bad off she was. "I think we need to get the doctor to take a look," I told her.

I nearly cracked up when she replied, as clear as a bell, "I don't know how you are going to get me down the steps to the car!"

She was serious, and she was right. With an orthopedic appliance on each leg and her being totally limp, it was a remark filled with comedy.

"No," I managed a chuckle, "we're going to let them come and get you in an ambulance."

"Okay."

Nine-one-one is a sobering number to dial. The weight of the moment grew as the phone on the other end rang and then rang again.

"Nine-one-one, what is your emergency?"

"I have a medical emergency and need an ambulance at my location," I said, giving the address.

"Please describe the emergency."

"I have a fifty-year-old female in distress. She is having difficulty breathing and is becoming cyanotic."

Her cyanotic state, or bluish skin discoloration, indicated a lack of oxygen to her tissues. My early thoughts were that she'd had or was having a heart attack.

As the ambulance was dispatched, I hung up the phone, turned to my wife, and told her, "Let's pray."

I don't recall the exact words I prayed as I leaned close to her face and drew her to me, but they expressed my smallness and inability to understand how to act effectively during such an overwhelming time. I sensed somehow that I must not tell God what I wanted Him to do but that I must trust Him to do whatever His will was.

It was in that moment that I gave Carolyn completely into God's hand. Whether she would live or die was not something I could influence, but I could trust that whatever the outcome, God's perfect will would be done. I could ask no more than that. I can only say that even that prayer came from outside me because I don't believe that I had the spiritual wisdom on my own to let go of my wife and give her up completely.

Tim took a flashlight to the street to help the ambulance driver in locate our house. I stayed in the room with Carolyn. When the

EMTs arrived, they asked the questions they needed to ask while they were collecting vital medical information. I moved across the room, out of their way. I noticed that they began to whisper and had an air of heightened concern. Her blood pressure was not measurable one moment, and then it would return. She was in real trouble.

The decision was made to transport her as quickly as possible even though she was not yet stable, which was a concern. I watched as they loaded Carolyn into the back of the ambulance. As quickly as the door closed, I got into my car and sped to the hospital. Because the ambulance was unable to turn around in the narrow street, the driver had to go around the block, which meant I had time to arrive at the emergency room just before the ambulance did. As the ambulance pulled up, I approached the back of the ambulance, where one of the EMTs told me, "Excuse me, sir," in a firm tone that communicated this was not a time for hand-holding. Carolyn was failing, and fast.

I stepped back, watched the EMTs unload the stretcher bearing my wife, and fell in behind them as they hurried into the emergency treatment area of the hospital.

From the passageway outside the trauma room, the scene was like one from a movie. Everyone in the room was doing something. There was no standing around—just purposeful activity. The sensation of seeing all this activity yet not being part of it was that of being in another dimension and peering into this one. The detachment was surreal. My mind and emotions were starting to slip into a defensive mode, walling me off from all things painful.

A surgeon friend who was working that night looked up, and realizing who I was and that this was not an area where people who didn't have business at the hospital would normally be, he asked if I needed anything and if I would like to have a seat. My response was more acquiescence than agreement. He wisely asked one of the ER staff to lead me to the waiting room and assured me that they would keep me informed. Time passed, and then a nurse came to me in the waiting room and through her own tears, told me that the preliminary assessment was that Carolyn had suffered a pulmonary embolism. I knew what the term meant, but that was all. The nurse's difficulty in maintaining her composure told me more than I really wanted to know; things were far more serious than I could have ever imagined.

It occurred to me that I should call family and friends. Our son Chris was the first one to call. He and Brandi dropped three-month-old Will off at his other grandparents and rushed to the hospital. Next I thought I should call Carolyn's parents, but I wondered if that was a good idea because I knew there was nothing they could do and that they would not sleep again that night. *What if she dies?* I thought. *How would they feel if I didn't at least let them know Carolyn was ill?*

So the call was made. I suggested it might be better if they waited at home since a trip to the hospital late at night would just be an added physical drain for us all. They graciously agreed.

For several years Carolyn had met weekly with two friends to pray together. Theirs was a bond forged through many hours together, and I needed them to know what was going on. I called Beth because her phone number was easy to remember. I told her the situation and asked her to call Rosemary and pray for Carolyn.

Chris arrived at the ER, and I told him what I knew. His presence was a tremendous comfort since he was certified as an EMT and had worked as one even though he was no longer employed in the field. I knew I would be able to rely on his knowledge and experience. Having both of my sons with me was so important to me.

I have no idea how much time—thirty minutes to an hour maybe—elapsed before a doctor asked us to meet with him in a conference room. Dr. Jeff Evans, the pulmonologist on call that night, was a personal friend with whom I had attended Promise Keepers conferences. My visual memories of the events by this time were images viewed through a haze as fuzzy outlines. Jeff's face was not visible to me either because my focus was not on him or because of the haze, but I heard him begin, "Gary, we think Carolyn has had a massive pulmonary embolism."

In shock, I didn't know how to respond or what to ask. Chris, who was seated on my right, asked, "What is the prognosis?"

Jeff replied, "It's too early to say for sure. She may not make it through the night . . ."

I was paralyzed.

"She was without oxygen for so long that if she does make it," he continued, "we don't know what level of brain function to expect. But it is also possible she could just walk out of here."

My mind was numb. What if Carolyn pulled through the initial crisis, only to be in a persistent vegetative state! How would I ever be able to care for her? It was close to being more than I could bear. I was certain that none of the answers to these questions would be affordable, either financially or emotionally. What would I do?

In a moment hardly described as one of clarity, I realized consciously that she was still my wife and that for what it was worth, I would do whatever I had to do to care for her. That had been my promise to her, and if God would give me the strength, I would honor that promise.

The rest of the meeting with Jeff Evans was beyond what I could absorb, and I have no recollection of it. At some point Jeff asked me if I would like to see Carolyn, and that ended the conference. Someone escorted me to a room where they had stabilized Carolyn and were assisting her respiration since she was unable to breathe on her own. She had the look of death. Her eyes were closed, and she was motionless. Her skin was unlike anything I had ever seen on a living person—darker than usual with a purplish marbling—but she was alive, and I was thankful for that.

I am certain that if Jeff had not been called in, Carolyn would not have lived through her time in the trauma room, but not because she did not receive appropriate care, because she certainly did.

When Jeff arrived, after being called in, he immediately recognized Carolyn and already knew what her recent medical history had been, so he knew what the root of her problem was and how to lead the medical team. Along with that, Jeff and I had met together with two others over several months for coffee and prayer and had developed a special kind of friendship. It was that relationship that pushed him to continue their efforts to resuscitate Carolyn much longer than likely would have been the case. In fact, weeks later I remembered what Jeff had said in one of our prayer times much earlier, "Since moving to Oxford, I haven't had to treat anyone I know as an emergency patient, but I know one day I will."

Weeks later we were talking and Jeff told me, "I didn't know who it was when I got the call, but when I came in the door and saw her feet, I froze, because I knew exactly who it was. Then my training just kicked in, and we did what we had to do." I have thanked God many times for Jeff, his training, and those who assisted him.

Carolyn was taken to the ICU on the third floor at around midnight. I waited in the hallway outside while they transferred her to a bed and made the necessary connections to the respirator and monitors. Things were still a blur, and my mind was racing. Although I can't recall who appeared first, people started popping up.

To my left from inside the ICU waiting room Jeff's wife, Laura, emerged. Beth and Rosemary had come earlier, and the three of them were praying for Carolyn. Robert Allen, one of the ministers at our church, had come when someone notified him and other ministerial staff. It was late, but they were all on hand. Chris had contacted my close friend and prayer buddy James, but he had not found us in the ICU and returned home and began praying for us there. I had released Carolyn into God's merciful hands but continued to pray that He would heal her and restore her perfectly.

When the respirator and monitoring equipment were in place, Jeff let me into the ICU to be with Carolyn. She was asleep, as she would be for several days. Jeff told me that she was stable, but his experience was that it would likely be seventy-two hours before we would really know which way things were headed. Things were settling down now as the first hurdle—stabilization—had been cleared. Now we would wait.

I waited in the ICU at Carolyn's bedside. Her nurse, Debbie, quietly and efficiently came and went. I was impressed and comforted by her kindness to both Carolyn and myself. I was allowed to stay beside Carolyn, holding her hand and alternately praying for and speaking to her from my chair. Occasionally I laid my head on the bed and catnapped. I was exhausted.

The next morning, June 7, I came home to clean up, get a bite to eat, and see my mother—and father-in-law before returning to the hospital. While there, I sent the e-mail message at the beginning of this chapter to every person in both our address books without regard to their faith. The only avenue available to us was prayer, and we appreciated every prayer that would be offered. Over the days and weeks to come, we heard from old friends and total strangers alike as they expressed their support for us. It was overwhelming that so many would stop what they were doing, pray, and even return a message of encouragement. Since then whenever I receive a prayer request by e-mail, my personal response has been to stop whatever I am doing and pray right then. The next message I sent follows:

Subject: God Has Heard
Date: Tue, 08 Jun 1999, 23:27 (11:27 p.m.)
From: Gary and Carolyn Carter
To: (recipients)

Dear Friends,

You have all been so kind to lift Carolyn in prayer. These last two days have been without comparison.

Without you having to read the following in suspense, let me say now that Carolyn has been the recipient of the grace of God in such a way as I cannot adequately describe. Simply put, she has experienced miraculous recovery that has gripped all who have heard of her condition.

The message I sent you earlier was posted at about 10:00 a.m. Monday. I have learned so much about pulmonary embolism since then. Most people do not recover from an episode such as Carolyn experienced. Those who do never experience such dramatic improvement at the startling rate she has seen. On Monday at 6:00 a.m., she was aware but not alert. She was nominally responsive. By noon she was active, recognizing all of us and responding to questions by hand-squeeze (she was on a respirator). Her condition improved noticeably at every visit to ICU (two-hour intervals).

On Tuesday by 8:00 a.m., they removed her respirator and tube and removed her feeding tube, and we have been able to continue to observe an astounding rate of recovery every visit. Tonight at 8:00 p.m., she has been asking when we thought we might be able to go home!

My medical friends have told us that there is no description outside of miraculous. We have seen mercy and favor from the hand of God—and seen it in a way that is unmistakably and uniquely His. We are awed and humbled that He would allow us to be used in a way that glorifies His name in such a powerful way.

Carolyn has come light years in a very short time. She still has a way to go, but we believe that God has not brought her this far to leave the task unfinished. We thank Him for honoring the prayers of so many believers, some of whom we have not even met. He has shown Himself to be faithful, intimately involved in our affairs, and willing to touch the life of one who will call out to Him in faith. Please continue to pray for Carolyn. We know that He is not forced into action by a prayer formula but has graciously and superabundantly responded to the fervent prayers of men and women who have sought Him on our behalf.

We thank you and bow before a loving Father, the Sovereign God, who has responded to the cries of His children for another.

We ask that His name may be glorified by what He has done. We ask God's blessing of peace on each of you and that you may be strengthened by knowing of His mighty deeds.

Gratefully,
Gary Carter

As Carolyn began to be increasingly alert, it was better for her to rest between the prescribed visiting times. During a Monday visit, she looked at me through groggy eyes and began to move her hand in something of a circular pattern. This was harder than it sounds, since her wrists were in restraints to prevent her from accidentally grabbing at an IV. Taking a stab at what she was doing, I asked, "Do you need something?" She nodded slowly. "Do you want to write something?" She looked relieved that I had understood and again nodded slowly.

The doctor quickly took out his pen, and we found a piece of paper. Holding the paper under her hand, we watched as she slowly scrawled "B-e-t-h" and "R-o-s-e-m-a-r-y."

"Do you want to know if Rosemary and Beth know you are here?"

She nodded, and I replied that they knew and that they were in the waiting room. Again the hand movement.

"Do you want them to come in?" I looked at the doctor, and he nodded that it was okay. I went to the waiting room and brought in the two women. Her recognition of her two friends was obvious. They only stayed a moment, but we knew from the encounter that even though she was still under some effects from the drugs used to keep her unconscious earlier, a high level of awareness was present.

Dr. Evans had cautioned that it would be seventy-two hours before we would know much but maybe this was an early indication. The day was spent mostly in the waiting room between visits with Carolyn and visiting those friends who were beginning to appear as the word got out.

Earlier on Monday morning, I called my brother, Ronnie, who lived about four hours south of our home. His wife, Rita, answered. She was a school teacher and still at home, preparing to leave for a continuing education workshop out of town. When Rita asked if there was anything she could do, I told her things were still up in the air but I would keep in touch. She told me Ronnie, a state trooper, was out of the state at a training workshop but that she would let him know. She, too, was shaken by the news from the early-morning phone call.

Rita called back later to tell me that she and Ronnie were both coming and that she would arrive before Ronnie since he would be driving from Indiana. I had not considered asking them to come, but they dropped everything to be here. When Rita arrived, it was such a relief to have family nearby, especially a woman who could take charge of household things. I still laugh that when we put sheets on the guest bed, she asked, "Do y'all like the pattern facing up toward the blanket or down facing the fitted sheet?"

She was giving me a lot more credit than I deserved in managing the homey side of a house, especially since my decision-making abilities had recently been depleted.

"However you do it, that's the way I do it," I answered. I don't remember how we did it; I just know it was the way she did it.

On Tuesday morning, I went down to the hospital to be on hand early for the 8:00 visit. A longtime doctor friend of my in-laws was making his hospital rounds, and though not involved with Carolyn's case, he had looked in on her. When he entered the waiting room and saw me, he moved to where I was with quick, long strides.

"Gary, it is an absolute miracle," he exclaimed as he took my hand and embraced me. "What you would expect to see in a person pulled from the bottom of a lake after twenty-five minutes is what you should expect to find in Carolyn," he said, and paused, ". . . but it's just not there!"

They had not yet allowed me into ICU because Carolyn's doctors were seeing her, which I understood. What I didn't know at that time was that Dr. Evans had determined that she was able to breathe without the respirator and had removed it. A major milestone had been reached eighteen hours after Carolyn entered ICU. I could hardly grasp the importance of the moment.

On entering the ICU, I found Carolyn awake, though she appeared to still be waking up. She smiled. I beamed! I moved quickly, deliberately to her side and gently took her hand.

"Hey," I said softly and smiled at her. That's when the fun began, though I'm not sure I was as amused at the time.

116

As I leaned close to Carolyn, she looked up and asked with a raspy croak, "What happened?"

I remembered that she might have brain damage, so without going into a lot of detail, I explained that she had had a serious medical emergency Sunday night, had been rushed to the ER, and was still in the hospital. I assured her she was much better and that we were awfully glad to have her back. All the while I was telling her this she was watching me intently and nodding in apparent understanding.

As I finished telling her this simplified version, she made a final nod of her head, and without shifting her gaze, asked, "What happened?" I repeated the explanation once more only to have her inquire yet again, "What happened?"

Fortunately Dr. Evans was there to assure me that this was expected and probably not long-lasting. It is today a two-word punch line that speaks volumes, especially when delivered with just the right croak, "What happened?" We learned shortly that the croaky voice was the result of the intubation. It lingered, but after months of voice therapy, it eventually subsided.

Wednesday was marked by continued improvement even to the point of Carolyn being moved from ICU to a private room. Although Carolyn has a positive and happy personality to begin with, throughout all this time Carolyn was uncommonly cheery and polite. We all got a laugh at her expense when Rosemary recalled a visit and mocked her for a syrupy, "It was so nice of y'all to come and see me. I hope you will come and see me again." It was good to be able to laugh. It was good, too, to have friends who were so supportive.

At some point during Carolyn's recovery, after the broken bones but before the embolism, I remembered having heard a preacher answering the often-asked question, "Why does God allow hard things into our lives?" I haven't been able to rediscover who that preacher was, but he surely offered some great answers. The answers took on fresh meaning when we found ourselves dealing with hard things.

Sometimes God uses hard things to chasten us when we have become disobedient or prideful or have otherwise acted in a way to deserve them. Too often that is where we stop looking for answers and assume we are simply getting our just desserts. We sometimes encounter hard things so God may use them to build our character. We may also face hard things and gain the experience that helps us to minister to others to whom we are credible because we have been where they are. The last is what Carolyn and I believed was true early on.

We had already learned something about life with disabilities, but while driving to the hospital on Thursday, I had not driven even a block when as surely as if it had been audible, I understood the unspoken, "That My glory may be manifest." There was no voice— just the realization of this unmistakable truth.

There had been such a clear and powerful manifestation of God's glory that people all over the hospital were talking about this miraculous recovery. Each day Carolyn regained more of her strength. Each day she regained more of the memory that had been sketchy and fleeting earlier.

Just before lunch on Monday, June 14, Dr. Evans came into the room with a big smile and asked, "Do you want to go home?" Carolyn was released from the hospital with instructions to make office visits to Dr. Lowe and Dr. Evans. Both appointments were in early July, and both doctors were pleased to see the progress that Carolyn continued to make. And who wouldn't be? Both of these men knew how close death had come. When Carolyn asked them whether she would be able to continue her plans for a second career as a classroom teacher, both offered the same thought: "Sure you will; just not anytime soon."

Roughly a month later, Carolyn stood before her first class at Davidson Elementary School in nearby Water Valley, Mississippi by God's amazing grace and so God's glory might be made manifest.

# CHAPTER 12

# BETH AND ROSEMARY
# MY PRAYER PARTNERS

## BETH'S RECOLLECTIONS

Carolyn did well despite her two broken legs. The fall over the water hose in the driveway had done a number on her active lifestyle, but despite being a little immobile, she maintained her good-spirited nature and adjusted as best she could to life with propped-up legs, wheelchairs, and walking canes. It's harder when one breaks both legs because there is nothing to lean on, so to speak.

Once the orthopedic boots were off, she still had to be careful as she got used to the new tingling in her legs, but she seemed to be headed full speed toward healing when something happened that Sunday night that changed it all.

DeDe, my husband, and I had mellowed into the night when the phone rang. I could hear a controlled panic in Gary's voice on the other end of the line. "Beth, the ambulance is here. They are rushing Carolyn to the emergency room. Something is very wrong; she is not breathing well. Please pray. This is serious," he said. "Yours was the only number I could remember. I've got to go!"

Rosemary, Carolyn, and I had had prayer time weekly for more than fifteen years. We had come to depend upon the prayers of the other two when one of us was down. It's really such a testimony to God's love and provision for His children that God always seemed to bolster up two of us when the other one would need to be propped up in prayer. We had come to realize over the years that sometimes when trials hit one's life, there really are no words. The pain, the confusion, and the heartache are so intense that we can only offer God the soft groanings of the Spirit because the words will not come as we rely on the power of intercessory prayer by those who love us.

So it would be this time as well.

I turned to DeDe and said, "I've got to go; I'll call you as soon as I know something. Love you. Bye!" Then I ran out the door.

As I rushed to the ER, the night seemed stagnant and strangely calm. It was one of those Mississippi nights where the wind barely stirs. I slammed the car into park and ran for the emergency room entrance, scanning the room for sight of Gary, Tim, or Chris.

Gary was sitting with his hands clasped together; the boys were hovering nearby. Gary rose when he saw me come in, and I saw the look in his eyes. It's interesting how a Christian reacts to tragedy. There was stress and fear in his eyes, but at the same time, I saw calmness, a light of hope that others who don't believe in the power and love of God can't understand. Gary knew that now we all were depending on God more than ever before to intervene—somehow, some way.

Gary said that about an hour earlier Carolyn had complained about cramping in one of her legs and had asked Gary to massage the cramp out. Gary has always had such a servant spirit for anyone in need, so he put aside the normal after-church panorama of things to do and sat down in front of Carolyn to try to ease the pain in her right leg. After a few minutes of massaging, Gary said Carolyn had felt a little better as she wheeled her wheelchair back to bed to get ready for bed. Within minutes, however, the "better" changed.

As I scanned the emergency room, I saw Carolyn had already been rushed to the back. I didn't know at that point that Carolyn had stopped breathing. About that time, one of the nurses came to get Gary and the boys to take them to the family prayer and conference room. Gary asked me to come in with them, and in a few minutes, the doctor walked through the door and addressed Gary.

"Carolyn has experienced a pulmonary embolism and has stopped breathing," Dr. Jeff Evans, the pulmonary doctor and one of our friends from First Baptist Church, said. I could see the look in Jeff's eyes. There was confidence and determination but also a sense of dependency on God that we could feel. Jeff depended on his expertise in medicine, but more important was the fact that the strength and wisdom for what he did so well was vested in the God he loved and served. Jeff told Gary that the situation looked grave and that even if Carolyn lived, she would probably have permanent, irreversible brain damage. Jeff prayed with us and then left to hurry back to Carolyn. We found out later that Jeff indeed had refused to give up on Carolyn. Although she had stopped breathing, he did continual CPR for more than twenty-five minutes.

Gary and the boys went with Jeff while I stayed and knelt to pray that our God would spare my friend's life. I slipped out to call Rosemary, and after I told her about the severity of the situation, she simply said, "I'm on my way."

When friends are bonded through a love higher than the love this world provides, there is a unity of mind and spirit that calls us to pray.

It goes deeper than the customary, "I'll check with you later" attitude. We would need to come through the long hours of that night into what the Lord calls "effective, fervent prayer" (James 5:16 NKJV). As it turned out, what we experienced that night in prayer would change my prayer life forever.

Rosemary arrived, and shortly after that, the medical staff moved Carolyn to intensive care. Rosemary and I found our spot in the ICU waiting area. It was a spot God had prepared for us: a little cubbyhole of a room with a window that looked out on the waiting area and toward the door to the ICU wing itself. It was a quiet spot. Others would have had to turn a corner or two to find us, so we settled in to pray. We knew God had called us there for that purpose and that purpose only. Gary and the boys knew of our concern for them, but by now, God had filled the room with our pastoral staff and friends who had heard the news and come to comfort and help. Gary and the boys were in good hands—God's hands and those of many loved ones—so Rosemary and I pulled up our chairs to talk with God privately.

When I had run from the house earlier, I grabbed a little stand-up promise calendar Rosemary bought for me while she was on vacation. Now I pulled it from my purse, and we placed it before us in the dim light of the little room. We began to claim the promises of God written there on behalf of our friend. As we would read a promise, God would flood our minds with the things we must pray for our sister in Christ. The words just kept coming . . . and coming.

We could hear the updates the staff was giving Gary from behind our little window in the room. Those details would help us pray more specifically for the wisdom of the team of doctors and nurses working on Carolyn and would pull us to the throne of God as we asked for a miracle for our friend.

The Bible says to pray while believing, and something God had given us in our spirits would not allow us to lose hope. God could do this! God could save Carolyn's life! Not knowing His perfect will, but resting in God's love and power toward His children, we continued to pray.

There have been times before when I had cried before God, pleaded with God, and poured my heart out to Him, but I can honestly say that this night was different. God's Spirit was with us in that little room as I had never sensed it before. "For where two or three are gathered together in my name, I am there in the midst of them." (Matt. 18:20 NKJV). He was there that night; we felt His presence.

I have no idea how long we prayed—hours, I think. It was one of the few times in my life when I *knew* fervent prayer was needed and God was calling us to obey. He was there listening to every word we uttered. God had laid a foundation of knowledge for the three of us years before. Our little prayer group had long ago learned the concept of praying in one accord—really praying as the other one voices that prayer, not just listening, and not just thinking of what to pray next. The unity of Spirit causes something like the merging of many waters into a flood of power to flow from those who intercede for one they love to the God who holds us in His arms.

That night, we prayed specifically, tagging on to each other's prayers and asking for help on Carolyn's behalf as God blended our hearts together with His. The spirit helped us to know what to pray—just like the Bible says (Rom. 8:26). The thoughts and needs, of course, were given to us by God Himself, for He had a mighty plan for our friend.

I don't remember the exact words we said as we prayed. It was as though our little table (by now with several cups of coffee scattered around it) was a stage, and God was our audience. He would give us the cues, prompt us with the Scripture, and pull from us the intensity of fervent prayer.

Sometime during the night, Gary had told us to go home and rest. The family members were exhausted and trying to drape themselves across the small chairs in the ICU waiting room. Rosemary and I left reluctantly, with promises to return early the next morning.

Later the next day we received news that Carolyn was breathing on the ventilator. She was nonresponsive to stimuli around her and could not speak. But she had motioned to Gary, who was beside her bed, that she wanted to write something. In a scrawled, jagged script, she wrote, "Beth . . . Rosemary . . ." As her strength dwindled, Gary picked up the pen from her limp hand, knowing she was asking to see us, and he hurried to the ICU area to get us.

When we parted the curtain to enter Carolyn's room, she was pale and weak. She didn't move, but her eyes darted toward us as we appeared in the doorway. She tried to lift her hand toward us. Even though she could not say it in audible words, we knew what she was trying to say. She needed to know that we were praying for her, a fact of which we assured her. We held her hands and told her how God was going to prove Himself so mighty in this and that we would continue to lift her up. God would be the secure foundation she needed through the long weeks ahead.

Carolyn was not supposed to live, but even though she was still in critical condition, God had shown us that He was not ready to carry Carolyn home eternally just yet. We would watch as He continued to give her strength that no one thought she would ever have again.

The odds had been against our friend, but God doesn't play the odds. He holds them—and us—in His hands. And He still does so today. We—and you—can depend on Him.

## ROSEMARY'S RECOLLECTIONS

There are times in our lives when we just need to get away and rest. My husband, Greg, and I had just returned from the Smoky Mountains, and we were very rested. It was Sunday evening, and I was just getting ready for bed and ready to face the world on Monday morning happy and rested. And then the telephone rang.

Beth, one of my closest friends, prayer partners, and fellow coffee drinkers, was calling me from the hospital. She told me that Carolyn (also one of my closest friends, prayer partners, and fellow coffee drinkers) was in the hospital. I remember Beth's words: "I think they have lost her."

I remember thinking, *How do you lose someone in the hospital?* Then I returned to reality and asked her what she meant. She told me she that Carolyn had quit breathing. That was all I needed to hear. Greg and I hurried to the hospital.

The first thing we saw as we pulled into the parking lot was Carolyn's son, Tim, sitting on the curb of the parking lot with his head in his hands. I don't know if he was crying or praying—or both. There were quite a few people from our church standing around and talking. I left Greg there. Beth and I did what Beth and I do; we went away to pray for Carolyn. We went to the intensive care room, sat at a table, and prayed and prayed.

While on vacation, I had purchased little calendars of Bible verses for Beth and Carolyn with their names on the front. I had already given Beth her calendar but still had Carolyn's calendar in my purse, so I pulled Carolyn's out of my purse, and we prayed God's Word back to Him. I believe what the Bible tells us in the book of Isaiah that His Word will not return to Him void but will accomplish what He purposed. I am so glad I had that calendar. My own words failed me.

Later—I don't know how much later—we were asked if we would like to see Carolyn in intensive care. Of course we did. Beth and I talked to her and patted her hand and rubbed her arm. We told her that we loved her and were praying for her. I don't think Carolyn heard us, but that didn't matter. We would tell her later that we love her and prayed for her. I remember that the nurse asked us, as we were leaving, if we were her sisters. Beth is tall and blond, while I am short with dark hair, and Carolyn is short with brown hair. We certainly don't look like sisters! But it didn't matter. We are sisters in the Lord.

As we were driving away from the hospital, I so much wanted her to wake up and hear her say (as she always does), "Hi, how you?" (Carolyn always leaves out the "are" in this greeting.) I didn't know what to expect the next day, but that didn't really matter. I knew she was in God's hands. I also knew that I wasn't ready for Him to take her home yet. Carolyn, Beth, and I still had a lot of praying to do and lot of coffee to drink. It also didn't matter to me that I was no longer rested. There would be other vacations to take. My priorities had changed. "Hi, how you?" was what I needed—much more than rest!

# CHAPTER 13

# DR. EVANS— WITNESS TO A MIRACLE

A real advantage to practicing medicine in a small town is that you get to know the people who are also your patients. This is also a disadvantage. One of the hardest things I have had to do since moving to Oxford, Mississippi, in 1994 is to provide care for those who became my friends, colleagues, or fellow physicians *before* becoming a patient.

In my residency, I developed a special bond with a patient named Jim (name changed for privacy), an elderly man who had a terminal disease. I would often go by and make a special visit just to chat because he had so many interesting things to say and was so entertaining. We made memories together, and he really enjoyed telling me stories about his kids and grandkids, the war and life in the good ol' days. Unfortunately, I was on call the night this gentleman developed his final diagnosis of internal bleeding, which would eventually lead to his death.

We are always told as physicians not to get too close to our patients, and as is often the case, we all learn better by experience than by instruction. When I was required to be Jim's doctor during that critical time, I found it very difficult to provide the care he needed and felt responsible in some way for whether he lived or died. Somehow my compassion for him as a person overwhelmed what I was able to offer him as his physician, and this left me with a terribly uncomfortable feeling.

I vowed after that experience that I would always keep my patients at arm's length and that I would stick to the task at hand of being the best doctor I could without getting intimately involved in their lives. In the practice of pulmonary and critical care medicine, this has proved a useful strategy for preserving my sanity, though at times I am perceived as more of a technocrat than a caring individual.

In today's world, practicing medicine is often more about the results or outcomes rather than about the care. Medicare expects compliance with core measures, those individual tasks that every person with a certain condition must get because it has been shown to improve mortality. Administrators expect you to keep everyone "very satisfied" with their care. Patients' families expect Momma to live forever, and most of us who live in the great United States somehow think we are invincible and immortal.

It seems that the expectations today's society places on doctors are more in the realm of miracle worker rather than that of a compassionate caregiver who took the Hippocratic Oath and only committed to two things: first, do no harm and second, prevent pain and suffering.

In my twenty-three years of practice, I have learned the balance between the technical aspects of my job and the compassion that is required to be a good doctor. This is not a human quality but more of a calling, like a ministry, if you will, that can only be effective through faith in God. In fact, I don't see how any physician can practice medicine without depending daily on the Creator of life itself. As I tell people often, "I am only an instrument to be used by God to accomplish His perfect will." Psalm 55:22 NASB says, "Cast your burden on the Lord and he will sustain you; He will never allow the righteous to be shaken." He is really always in control of everything!

That brings me to the night of Sunday, June 6, 1999, when I was called upon to care for one of my dear friends, Carolyn Carter. Call is really the drudgery of most doctors' existence. We hate it because it comes around regularly. and most of the time it results in what the rest of the world calls unplanned overtime. In 1999 there were three doctors in my group, meaning I was on deck for call every third night and every third weekend. A weekend meant taking all new admissions and problems from 5:00 p.m. on Friday until 8:00 a.m. on Monday.

The weekend of June 6, 1999, had been average, with about twenty-five patients in the hospital, six or eight of them on ventilators (life support) and in the critical care unit, with their associated crises, and a couple of ten-to twelve-hour days required to get the work done. I had gotten home around seven o'clock that evening and had my dinner, visited with my wife and two boys briefly, and then went to bed around 10:30.

There seems to be some sort of trigger that occurs every time I lay down in bed that causes my pager to go off. This night was no different. Go to sleep, answer a page, give orders, go back to sleep, repeat the cycle. I had probably gotten about one hour of uninterrupted sleep when I got a call from my colleague in the emergency department (ED) regarding a fifty-year-old lady who had sustained a cardiopulmonary arrest and required a twenty-minute resuscitation effort, only to be left with a very low blood pressure and continued low oxygen levels despite being on the ventilator.

He suggested that there really wasn't much else to do and that she would likely die, but for now we just needed to get her out of the ED to make room for other sick patients who were arriving. His comments to me were not atypical or unusual except for the age of the patient, which caught my attention because she was so young compared to most of my patients who are in their sixties, seventies, and eighties. I didn't even ask the woman's name since I knew I was going straight to the ED, and I figured I would just meet her there. I got out of bed, got dressed, and gave my wife a kiss.

She asked, "How long do you think you will be?"

I responded, "'Bout an hour or so," which would be the typical time frame for the situation.

The emergency department of most hospitals is usually characterized by a hustle and bustle of seemingly chaotic activity. Patients and various medical personnel scurry about with a sense of hurriedness to produce a diagnosis and execute proper treatment. This night was no different, and upon my arrival in the ED, the attending physician there was exiting the woman's room and met me on my way in. He reiterated the details of the case with me, but as he spoke, I could not keep my eyes from focusing on the two orthopedic boots that were on both of the patient's legs and suspended in the air, while her face was not visible because she was in the trendelenburg position to try to maintain blood pressure. "I've seen these boots before," I said to myself, "recently . . ."

Curiosity and my inability to make the connection drew me into the room, where I saw my friend Carolyn in critical condition, cyanotic in color, completely unresponsive to pain stimulus, with an endotracheal tube in place, and connected to a ventilator. Her blood pressure was extremely low, and her oxygen saturations were not normal, which relates to an ongoing loss of brain cells despite a successful resuscitation. I had seen those boots earlier that week when I saw Carolyn at church, riding around in a wheelchair after sustaining a fracture of a bone in the lower right leg and fractures in the left foot.

I actually knew Gary, Carolyn's husband, better than I knew her. We went to church together, and Gary and I had been in an accountability group with a couple of other guys. Through this relationship, we had gotten to know a great deal about each other and our families. We had taken a "deep dive" to strengthen our relationships with our Christian brothers and our families, so I knew a lot about what Gary thought about his wife and how very special their relationship was. He is a great example of what a loving husband is, and I knew he would likely be devastated if Carolyn didn't pull through.

My first response was disbelief, but a quick face check and a review of the demographic page confirmed that this was indeed Carolyn

Carter, and overall things didn't look good. My first fear was that she wouldn't even live long enough to get to the ICU. My second fear was that if she did survive more than a few hours and become stabilized, she certainly would have a severe brain injury and live the rest of her life in a vegetative state.

In the practice of critical care medicine, there are times when death is truthfully more merciful than living. I prayed briefly for the Lord's will to be done and selfishly for my own strength to be able to minister to Carolyn's family through this event regardless of the outcome. I then drew upon my medical training to see that every base had been covered.

The most likely diagnosis was pulmonary embolus, which is fairly common in patients with immobility and especially more common in patients with orthopedic injuries. Venous blood pools in the affected extremities and then forms clots in the veins of the legs. Small pieces of clot then break off from the veins in the legs and circulate into the right heart and then into the main pulmonary arteries, leading to shortness of breath and a decrease in oxygen levels. If the clot is large enough, it can also cause impairment in blood flow through the heart, low blood pressure, or even sudden death.

In pulmonary emboli with hypotension or cardiopulmonary arrest, the prognosis is extremely poor and mortality approaches 80 percent. Of the 20 percent who survive, brain injury is common.

I reviewed the code sheet, a record that describes every intervention of the resuscitative effort, including CPR, drugs given, fluids administered, etc., and saw that she had not received any heparin, a blood thinner that is used to treat clots in the legs and lungs. I ordered a dose intravenously, and having satisfied myself that all that could be done had been done, I mustered up the courage to speak to the family.

I asked the ED nurse to find Gary and have him come into the back hall, away from all the chaos, so I could break the news to him. He seemed surprisingly calm and businesslike, and we shared a moment of bonding before getting into the conversation. I explained to him that Carolyn was very ill, that her chances for survival were poor, and that her chances of being the Carolyn he had grown to love and adore were even poorer. He expressed understanding and a sense of acceptance in a way that gave me great comfort and strength to fight harder for her life.

I went back to the trauma room where Carolyn was and noticed that she was gaining ground. Her blood pressure was increasing, and her oxygen levels were creeping into the normal range. I ordered a continuous infusion of the blood thinner and then began to make preparations for transfer to the ICU.

I saw that many of our friends had begun to gather at the hospital, and I knew my wife would want to know what was keeping me. I called her and told her that I would be later than my predicted hour and that the critical patient was Carolyn Carter. I also told her it didn't look good and that I would be surprised if Carolyn made it through the night.

After the paperwork was done and a bed was assigned in the ICU, I accompanied Carolyn and the transport stretcher to the ICU. No diagnostic tests had been done to confirm the pulmonary embolus, and in my opinion, she was just too unstable to be carted around the hospital for tests. My clinical judgment would have to suffice in this case. Over the next few hours, I explained all of the details of the case, the difficult decisions that might have to be made, and the overall poor prognosis with the rest of the family and our friends who were present. My one hour turned into an all-night affair. I left the hospital at 6:30 a.m. to get a quick shower and start my Monday.

The usual rule of thumb for brain recovery after cardiopulmonary arrest is that any meaningful recovery will be seen within forty-eight to seventy-two hours after the event. Carolyn's recovery was nothing short of miraculous. By Monday afternoon (just fifteen to eighteen hours after the initial event), she was awake, trying to talk, and making purposeful movements. She still had a high oxygen requirement and wasn't ready to be removed from mechanical ventilation, so some sedative medications had to be given so she could rest through the night.

By Tuesday morning she was able to be extubated (the removal of the tube used in intubation) and was able to speak coherently to me and Gary. By Wednesday morning, she was stable enough to move out of ICU, and on June 14 (just eight days after her cardiopulmonary arrest), she was discharged from the hospital on oral blood thinners and without oxygen, which, in my opinion was a truly remarkable recovery.

This experience is testimony to the fact that our thoughts are not always God's thoughts. What seems to make sense based on human opinion and research may not at all be what God intends. When you are faced with dismal circumstances, He will get you through them by giving you strength to endure or by showing His power through miraculous resolution. He will accomplish His will regardless, and through all things, He will be glorified.

We should allow ourselves to conform to His leading and live by faith, allowing Him to use us as His instruments. I know I had very little to do with Carolyn's survival and her complete recovery, but I was humbled and honored to be a witness to the miracle.

# CHAPTER 14

# RETURNING TO MY EARTHLY HOME

My experience that Sunday night was very much like that of a newborn baby—except just the opposite. I was thrust into a situation with people giving orders and talking very loudly, bright lights glaring, chest compression crushing my ribs, a breathing bag pumping the breath of life back into my body, and holes being punched all over me to admit the needed fluids to hydrate my body. At that point, I was feeling the love of no one except the accepting, loving arms of my heavenly Father.

The team didn't have time to love patiently; they were actively trying to save my earthly life. During this trauma, I slipped through heaven's birth canal and was escorted by angels into the arms of our Father. I left the trauma, the fear, and the pain behind. I was surrounded by warmth and love like I have never felt before. There were no more loud noises, no more bright lights, and no more panic. I could literally feel the arms of our loving God surrounding me with the joy and love that comes from the birth of a baby. I was, at that point, His baby being accepted and welcomed into His world. He accepted me with such joy that I felt like I was home at last.

My eyes were opened to a world that cannot be adequately explained in human words. I had read in the Scriptures that the glory of His face shone around Him. I witnessed that glow and radiance firsthand. I heard His voice. He spoke with a calm, soothing tone that I looked forward to hearing for eternity. I loved His world! "How lovely is Your dwelling place; O lord of Hosts! My soul longs, yes, faints for the courts of the Lord; my heart and flesh sing for joy to the living God" (Ps. 84:1-2 NASB).

God was allowing me to participate in an awesome experience that would change my earthly life forever. Sure, I had worried about what would take place after death. I knew I was saved and would go to heaven, but often I heard deep discussions in church about what happens immediately after death takes place. Some would say that the person would go immediately into the presence of God, while others would say you would need to wait until He chose to accept you. Now I know that all who have accepted Him as Lord and Savior will go directly into His presence, and your cares, pain, and worries are left behind. There were no tears there; only songs of joy. Heaven holds a warmth of joy and love so deep that death should be feared by no one who has accepted Jesus Christ as his or her Lord and Savior.

While my happiness and joy abounded, He told me in His calm, soft voice that I must return to the family and friends I had left on earth. He said that my purpose for living on earth had not been fulfilled and I must return. My heart was broken! I begged our Holy Father to please let me stay with Him. He assured me that I would be with Him again someday; however, He still had things for me to accomplish on earth. I begged to stay. Remember His promises in John 16:22 NASB: "Therefore, you too now have sorrow; but I will see you again, and your heart will rejoice, and no one will take your joy away from you."

I was kept in a drug-induced coma for several days, with brief periods of awareness to check my breathing patterns. If I seemed unable to breathe on my own, I was again sedated heavily and kept alive by the machine that was my lifeline. Of course, during this time, my doctor and my family had no idea that God had told me I would return to this earth and regain my earthly life. They prayed and fought to try to bring life back into a lifeless body. My memory of this time is gone. God spared me so much fear and pain by allowing me to be in His presence during this stressful time instead of realizing what my body was going through. My last real memory was getting ready for bed on Sunday evening after Gary graciously had pampered me with a foot and leg massage and painted my toenails.

My first faint memory after that was five days after the embolism lodged in my lungs. I vaguely remember Gary filling out my menu in the hospital and telling me what they would bring for my lunch instead of asking me first. I protested quietly about the green beans, reminding him that I had just had green beans. I really hadn't, but somewhere in my memory green beans were not a desired lunch item.

Just days after the embolism, the doctor removed many of the tubes that entered my body. He had placed a central line into my chest just below my collar bone. The tubes ran into my heart to provide the needed medications to keep me alive. A nurse came into my room and told me that the day had come to remove the central line from my chest. She took both of my hands and placed them around the side rails. She then placed a rubber mouth guard in my mouth, took the tubing into her hand, and told me to prepare myself. She said that the pain would feel much like childbirth, but it wouldn't last quite as long.

So, with the count of one, two, three, she pulled with all her strength, and the lines tore through my body. Yes, it did feel like childbirth. I was sedated, but I have no trouble remembering the intense pain that accompanied those few seconds that were needed to remove this foreign object from my body. With the amount of Cumadin that had been added to my daily medication, the blood flowed freely, and the wound was bandaged securely. Within minutes, I was sleeping calmly and peacefully, appreciating the soothing effects of pain medication.

That same afternoon, Dr. Evans suggested that Gary get me up in a wheelchair to build my strength and test my memory. He told Gary that a short ride down the hallway might stimulate some recognition, and anything would be better than the lifeless form that had occupied the hospital bed. A nurse carefully helped him lift me from the bed and place me gently into the wheelchair. I remember him saying, "Let's roll into the bathroom so we can comb your hair."

Our trip began with the detour into the bathroom. I decided that I wanted to see what my hair looked like for myself. I slowly eased myself up using my weak arms and turned my head to look into the mirror. The shock was so great at the image in the mirror that I literally fell into the wheelchair and wept. My face had no color, and my eyes were sunken into their sockets. My hair was sticking up on all sides as Gary patiently tried to smooth the curls that had formed from days of lying in bed. My lips were cut from the tube that provided the breath of life during the first three days following the embolism. The tube had been placed in my mouth and taped securely to the sides of my cheeks. It cut into the bottom of my lips and formed sores that were now scabs both inside and on top of my bottom lip. I still couldn't comprehend what had happened to me, nor could I remember when my family and friends later tried to explain it yet again.

On the eighth day following the embolism, I was allowed to leave the hospital and go home. My memory was improving. Gary had tested my memory each day I was in the hospital by asking visitors to sign in when they arrived. I would visit with them and enjoy our time together. Then the following day, Gary would ask who came to see me the day before.

For the first three days, I would almost cry and answer, "No one." By the fourth day, I remembered that two people had been to see me, and by the sixth day, I was able to name four people who had visited in my hospital room. Oh, what an improvement! I guess you can call naming four out of twelve an improvement.

By the eighth day, I was remembering almost everyone who had been by and even remembering things that happened before my embolism. This was truly a miracle. I could talk and think. I could use my hands and hopefully use my legs when the breaks healed. The nurses and doctors who had attended me on Sunday night came to my room just to see the miracle that I had become. I received hundreds of hugs and best wishes when we left to go home through the front doors of the hospital.

My existence at home was back to my bed, my wheelchair, or my favorite chair in the den. I was very weak and had to practice to force my arms to lift me. The doctor had told Gary before I left the hospital that more blood clots remained in my right leg, so I was to remain as calm and quiet as possible and the clots would eventually dissolve with time. Both the doctor and Gary realized what a blessing the breaks were at this time, because I couldn't be too active. I was on strong doses of medication that made me bleed or bruise from just a touch.

Twice a week, Gary and I returned to the hospital for a blood test to check the clotting levels of my blood. My arms quickly looked like those of a drug addict, with holes and bruises all over them. However, I was happy to be alive and healing. I was happy that I had been spared the trauma and pain that my family and friends said they had experienced during this stressful week.

By the first week in July, the boots were removed, and I was allowed to walk again. I was amazed at how unstable my body was and that I couldn't even stand up without holding on to the bed or a wall. I was forced to use a walker. My physical therapy was to be done three times a week so I could get stronger quickly. My therapist remained by my side every minute. I hadn't been told that if the clots had not totally dissolved, one could break loose during therapy. The therapist was instructed to watch for confusion, dizziness, weakness, or bluing of the nails and lips. About every two minutes I would hear, "Are you feeling okay?" I didn't understand why he stayed with me constantly.

During my third visit, he explained that he was a trauma survivor himself and about the blood clots. A few years earlier, he had hit his head while swimming and remained under the water for too long. The paramedics performed the same life-saving techniques on him that they had on me. He was not supposed to live. I was not supposed to live. However, God knew I needed him during therapy to understand what had happened and what needed to take place.

My strength improved, and my body was healing as the therapy continued for the next four months.

My vocal cords had been torn during the intubation at the hospital. I talked like I had a baritone voice and a sore throat at the same time. My voice was no louder than a whisper. Voice therapy was prescribed, so I began seeing the senior therapist at the speech and hearing center at Ole Miss. I was a phenomenon because of my age. The therapist and students often saw children and young adults in voice therapy, but I was forty-nine years old. My therapy room had one wall of one-way glass. Twenty to thirty students would sit behind the wall during my sessions and take notes for the future. I was glad to help them learn, but the whole situation made me feel very awkward. My voice therapy lasted for about a year. I finished up the following summer with instructions never to sing a lot and never to whisper. Apparently, this can further damage the vocal cords.

By the second week of July, I was going to physical therapy three times a week, voice therapy twice a week, and Coumadin therapy, which required two trips per week to the hospital for testing. At least now I could walk with the help of a walker, so I felt much more independent. I had withdrawn both of my applications to teach in the fall, under the doctor's advice. My life would now revolve around therapy. I just kept thinking, *This too shall end!* Well, it didn't end, but it did change abruptly one day.

# CHAPTER 15

# TEACHING 101

On July 17, 1999, I received a phone call from a friend who taught first grade in Water Valley, a small community about twenty miles south of Oxford. She told me that a fellow teacher had just turned in her resignation and would be moving with her husband in just a few days. She insisted that I apply for the job. My response was laughter! Why would a principal hire me? I couldn't walk or talk and had never really taught before. But what would be the harm in trying?

I told Gary to get dressed because we were driving to Water Valley. I put on a really cute pantsuit and my required tennis shoe footwear, grabbed my walker, and off we went. Gary talked during the whole drive about me working too soon and why I shouldn't push myself. I assured him that I understood but told him that the experience of a job interview was a good thing.

When we arrived, I chose to leave my walker in the car, so Gary escorted me in. I introduced myself to Glenda, the school secretary, and she handed me the paperwork to fill out. Once that was completed, she showed me into the principal's office. I sat down quickly so he wouldn't see me wobble. I loved the experience and enjoyed our chitchat before he really asked me any pertinent questions. Why be nervous when it was just a practice run? Of course, the question finally did arise, "I notice that you talk very softly. Why is that?"

I tried to cut my answer short and just explain that I had been sick earlier in the summer. He pushed and probed for more. I finally ended up telling him the whole story about breaking my legs, a blood clot breaking loose in the veins in the ankle, and having a pulmonary embolism. Now the truth was out. My chances of teaching were surely not good.

He asked about my teaching experience. I told him that I had taught about four months at Happy House Kindergarten back in 1970 but that I had no other experience. Another black mark! Then he asked about my ability to walk the children back and forth to lunch, to the bathroom, and to recess. Before I answered, I asked where the playground was. He said it was across the parking lot and down a steep hill from the building where I would teach. Being truthful, I answered, "I'm not sure about recess. The lunchroom and bathroom should not be a problem." Another black mark!

So there I sat; I couldn't walk, I couldn't talk, and I had no experience. Things were not going my way. He thanked me for coming and told me, "I'll let you know."

Well, I knew what that meant, but I didn't really care. He had been so nice to me and at least let me get one interview under my belt. Gary was patiently still sitting in the outer office. He jumped up and introduced himself to the principal, and then we were on our way.

Gary and I were leaving the following morning for a trip to Gulfport, Mississippi, to see Gary's parents. Before leaving the house, I remembered that I had not taken a copy of my teaching license for my interview the day before. We would be driving right by Water Valley, so I could run it into the office without losing too much time on our drive. I copied the original and put it in an envelope.

About twenty minutes into our trip, we pulled up in front of the school in Water Valley. I told Gary that I would only be a minute and he could just wait in the car. As I walked into the office, Glenda rose from behind her desk. I handed the envelope to her and she said, "Do you have just a minute? Mr. Hill wants to see you." I couldn't imagine why he wanted to see me, but she called him over the intercom, and I took a seat in his office.

When he came in, he escorted me into his office and closed the door behind him. He said, "Mrs. Carter, I have been looking over your application and resume. I am really impressed with what I see, and your references highly recommend you. I know you have had some health problems and will be limited for a while. I am offering you a job as the sixth-grade math teacher. We will provide a sound system with a lapel microphone for your classroom and any other equipment that you might need.

"Mrs. Carter," he continued, "I am offering you this job for two reasons. One, I see that you are a member of the Pilot Club of Oxford. In my former school district, the Pilot Club was very instrumental in getting things done. If you are anything like them, I want you here. And two, I feel God wants you here too."

Needless to say, I was speechless! I had never expected to become a teacher this soon. The Water Valley District was such a wonderful, small, friendly district. "Yes, I'll take it," I said. Mr. Hill then informed me that school would be starting late that year. They were finishing up on their new kindergarten wing, so the first day of classes would be August 15. I would have about three weeks to prepare.

Mr. Hill asked me to follow him to the adjoining building where my classroom was located. He opened the door to a brightly lit room filled with student desks, a teacher's desk, and a file cabinet. The floors shone with a freshly waxed finish. Their glow was almost blinding from the sun bearing down through the wall of windows that made the room so inviting. He quickly collected the teacher's editions for the subjects I would be responsible for teaching. The social studies book was rather small and unassuming. However, the teacher's edition for sixth grade math was in three volumes and was accompanied by testing manuals, overhead transparencies, a remediation guide, and an enrichment guide. My heart was beating ninety miles an hour, and I doubted my ability to do this job.

Meanwhile, Gary was waiting in the car and was wondering what was taking so long. He finally became a little worried and went into the main office to ask about me. Glenda didn't tell him I had gotten the job; she only said, "She has gone to the other building with Mr. Hill. They should be back in a minute." Gary sat down to wait some more.

Mr. Hill and I entered the office with our arms loaded with books. The look on Gary's face was priceless! I stopped in front of Gary and said, "Gary, I would like for you to meet my *new employer*, Mr. Hill." Gary quickly rose to his feet and extended his hand with a smile the size of Texas. He was just as stunned as I was, but both of us knew that it was a prayer that had been answered by God. God had provided a teaching position for me in a small, caring community. A great opportunity lay ahead of me that only God realized at this time.

After making arrangements to sign my contract, have fingerprints taken, and become officially employed by the district, we returned to the car to continue our trip. I would be back at the school the following week to complete my paperwork. I spent the next five hours in the car reading through the teacher's editions for the subjects I would teach. The more I read, the more relaxed I became. I had taken care of all of the accounting for the jewelry store, so surely I could teach sixth graders how to use decimals and find the square root of a number.

Our visit in Gulfport would be our first since I had broken my legs and experienced the embolism. As we drove into the driveway, we were met with the open arms of Gary's parents, Jean and Van. Their questions flowed like water. "How are you feeling? How are you enjoying retirement? Are you tired from the trip? Can I get you something to drink?"

We tried to respond, but the questions were coming too fast. We finally had a chance to catch our breath and sit down in their beautiful home. After a few minutes, we told them about my new teaching job. Jean was delighted to share with me that Gulfport has an outstanding teacher store named School and Carnival Supply and we could visit there in the morning. Now I knew God had worked out the timing for my new employment. I received the job on my way to

Gulfport, and now I would be able to buy the needed supplies for my new classroom the next day in Gulfport.

School and Carnival Supply was a smorgasbord of treats for teachers and/or Mardi Gras participants. The shelves were full of birthday charts, math posters, reference books, and all of the support materials that a teacher would need. I spent about $250 that day so that I would be ready to prepare my classroom for the coming year when I got home from our trip. With each step, I was becoming more and more excited about becoming a real teacher.

The first day of school was set aside for registration and meeting the teachers. Parents could come anytime during the day to the classroom to complete forms that would allow their child admittance for the coming year. This was also a valuable time for the teacher to meet the students and begin the process of learning their names and personalities. I was nervous about the day and hoped I would do everything correctly. God was about to reveal the first reason for my presence at Water Valley Elementary School. Would I be able to meet His expectations?

Water Valley was blessed to have Reedy Acres, a satellite location for the Baptist Children Village in Jackson, Mississippi. The elementary—through high school-age children who lived on the beautiful lakefront property came from broken homes or homes where no one was able to care for them. Some of these children would return to their homes once a loved one regained good health. However, some children were there because they had no one to love them and take care of them. There were many cases of deserted children who had been left on the doorstep at night and were added as residents of Reedy Acres.

My first day at school started out well, and I was began to relax as I met the students who would fill the seats in my classroom. The excitement I saw in the children's faces added to my enthusiasm about the coming year. I took a quick break for a sandwich at lunchtime and then was ready to complete the day. Around 1:30 p.m., I heard footsteps coming through my door. I looked up from my desk to see a beautiful young woman who served as a house parent at Reedy

Acres accompanied by a twelve-year-old girl named Sonia (not her real name).

Sonia was tall for her age and wore clothes that looked like they had been painted on. Her jeans were skin tight, and her pink top was so low cut that not much was left to the imagination. Her face was plastered with heavy makeup, and her hair was ratted out and colored an unnatural shade of blonde. She had hickeys running up and down her neck. Her posture radiated the fact that she didn't want to be there and would refuse to like this school.

Sonia had been dropped off at Reedy Acres the night before by her prostitute mother. Her mother had explained that she no longer wanted Sonia around because she restricted her nightlife. This explained a lot about Sonia's clothing and her attitude. Being deserted and being told that you are unloved is a terrible burden for a child to bear. Her house parent was doing the best job she could to make Sonia's life as normal as possible. She was enrolling her in school and would purchase appropriate clothing after leaving the school that day. She assured me that Sonia would look like a different child the next morning.

The next morning, I greeted twenty-three smiling faces who entered my classroom with enthusiasm about the new school year. Then I greeted Sonia, who obviously didn't feel a part of this chatty crowd and was hoping someone would come to save her before the day began. She was dressed in brand-new clothes that made her look like a fashion model, but she still wore the heavy makeup and had the ratty-looking hair. She pulled away and turned her head as I approached her for a morning greeting. She just walked away without speaking and slipped into the seat of her empty desk.

We spent the next hour unpacking backpacks and putting away the supplies the students brought to school. We played community building games to enable the children to become familiar with each other, but Sonia refused to participate. Lunchtime came, and no one sat with Sonia. She picked at her food and sat silently, watching the other children whispering and chatting during lunch. No one spoke to her.

We returned to the classroom and wrote stories about our summertime activities. Sonia wrote about her summer but not a story that could be read to the class. She was very open and honest in her writing about the lifestyle her mother was teaching her. When graded hers, I commented on the only two positive things in her paper: her handwriting was beautiful and her punctuation was perfect. She was obviously a smart child but one who had been seriously misdirected by the one person she loved the most.

Several days passed, and still no one would talk to Sonia or sit by her in the lunchroom. She stood alone during recess and watched the other children play. My heart was breaking, and I wanted to help her so much. The old saying is so true: "You can lead a horse to water, but you can't make him drink."

I asked some of the other girls to sit by Sonia at lunch. They did as I asked but still didn't include her in their conversations. I asked others to work with her in groups, but she was ignored. The other girls were talking and playing with their friends and leaving Sonia out.

I was working at my desk one afternoon during recess and grading the many tests that had been given that day. All of the children in the sixth grade attended my math class during the day, so I graded 125 papers each time a test was given. As far as I knew, the world had stopped outside, and I was the only person on earth. I was concentrating so hard that I didn't see Sonia enter my room. She walked up to my desk and cleared her throat, which brought me back to the real world. With big tears in her eyes, she asked if she could talk with me. I stood up and led Sonia by the hand to a small table in the back of the room.

When I asked Sonia what was wrong, she immediately began to sob into her hands. Her shoulders shook with such force that I placed my hand there to comfort her. She looked up at me with mascara running down her face and said, "Mrs. Carter, why doesn't anybody like me? Why won't anyone talk to me or play with me during recess?"

I knew now that God wanted to use me to help with this lonely child. I silently asked God to give me the words that would comfort her heart and give her advice that would improve the quality of her life. I knew she was ready to hear the real truth about what made them shy away from her. I had never seen such brokenness in anyone's life before.

I took Sonia's hand and asked, "How would you react to a new girl who entered our classroom from a different country? She couldn't speak the same language and would wear different clothes than we do. She might bring food in her lunchbox that we normally don't eat. Would you run up to her and welcome her, or would you stand back because she is different from you?" Sonia admitted that she would not be able to talk with her and would be scared to try.

I used this as a way to explain to Sonia that her makeup and hair were foreign to the other girls. I asked her to see the other girls in her mind and ask herself, "Do I see anyone in the sixth grade who wears makeup yet? Do I see anyone who colors their hair and wears the same style that I wear?"

In Water Valley, the girls were still children in the sixth grade. They didn't wear makeup and often wore their hair in a ponytail. They enjoyed playing games and running outside on the playground. None of the girls had been taught the ways Sonia knew. I challenged Sonia to come to school the next morning with no makeup. I asked her to wash her hair and just comb it out in a cute pageboy style. Then I asked her to trust me and believe things could change.

That night I prayed fervently for God to answer my prayers for Sonia and give her the courage to make these major changes in her appearance. I prayed that God would open the eyes of the other children to be able to see the heart inside this lonely child who wanted to be accepted and be their friend.

When Sonia walked through the classroom door the next morning, all heads turned her way. She was beautiful! Her childlike smile made her face glow, and the soft color of her skin was radiant. The girls one by one got up from their desks and ran to the door. They were all chattering about her new look and stroking her soft blond hair. I think Sonia was a little overwhelmed at the acceptance she felt. When she was finally able to break away from the crowd around her, she walked up to me and put her arms around me. As she hugged me, she whispered, "Thank you, Mrs. Carter." She really didn't need to thank me as much as to say a prayer of thanks to our heavenly Father. She was not quite ready for that yet, but I was working on it.

Sonia wasn't the only child God put in my path that year. I was reminded over and over why God had allowed me to live. He not only allowed me to live but also gave me back the completeness of my body—my mind, my physical abilities, my family, and my heart. I have always had a deep love for children, and God was using that love to soothe the hurts in these children's lives.

Jason (not his real name) was a small child for his age. He was about the height of a normal fourth grader but living in a sixth-grade world. He was a preciously happy child who always saw the positive in everybody and everything around him. About two months after school began, Jason began sleeping in class every Monday. He was completely alert during the rest of the week, but Mondays were really hard for him. I would walk past his desk and tap on the edge of his desk to wake him from his deep slumber. He would sit up and last about five minutes before dropping back into a sound sleep. After about three weeks of his Monday siestas, I pulled him aside and told him I wanted to talk with him during recess. He smiled and complied. We sat at the back table, which was isolated from the classroom door.

I asked him why he was sleeping so much in class on Mondays and his reply was, "I don't know."

"Are you staying up too late on the weekends?" I asked.

"No, but I can't sleep good on the weekends," he responded. This response puzzled me, so I probed a little more.

"What keeps you from sleeping on the weekends?" I asked.

His response was totally unexpected and broke my heart.

He looked at me with his big brown eyes and said, "Well, I have to go to the casino with my dad on the weekends because there is no one to keep me. We go in his eighteen-wheeler truck. Those people won't let me come in, so my daddy makes me stay in the truck while he goes inside and gambles."

My emotions lodged in my throat, and I was unable to speak for a minute. I felt true anger against his dad and a desire to shelter this precious child from further harm.

When my voice returned, I asked Jason if he was totally alone for the whole weekend. He replied, "My dad comes out to check on me at least twice a day and brings me food."

By law in Mississippi, any time a child alerts you, knowingly or unknowingly, to some form of child abuse, teachers must report this to their principals. My gut instinct told me that this was child neglect, and I was so afraid for Jason. He loved his dad so much, and I didn't want him taken away, but on the other hand, he was being neglected. After much prayer, I did report my conversation to my principal, and that was the last I heard about this problem. Apparently the Department of Human Services must have talked with Jason's dad. Jason no longer fell asleep in class and returned to the happy, healthy child who had first walked into my class.

Along with all of the troubled and needy children who were in my care during the day, I also had children who brought laughter and joy into the lives of everyone around them. Susie (not her real name) was a straight-A student. She was bouncy and happy and had blonde curls cascading down her back. She had a cute sense of humor that could cut through the most serious moments. She kept our class in stitches and made learning so much fun for the rest of the class.

One morning Susie came bouncing through the classroom door. She came straight to my desk and said, "Mrs. Carter, I want you to meet my new imaginary friend, Bob." I acted like I was shaking Bob's hand and told him that I was glad he was visiting in school that day. I really was hoping Susie would forget about her friend and life could move on.

She moved a small chair next to her desk so Bob could sit next to her. The bell rang, and the time had come to start multiplying a three-digit number by a three-digit number. The students opened their books to the correct page while Susie ran to the back of the room to get a book for Bob. I went over the process with the students and then asked several students to work problems on the board. Susie happened to be one of those students. She asked if Bob could go to the board with her. I said, "No, Bob is just here visiting." She pouted a little but worked her problem perfectly.

As the morning progressed, Bob went everywhere Susie went. He went to music class and sang with everyone. He went to the lunchroom with our class and had to have a seat next to Susie. He went to recess and played with all the children. As we were coming in from recess, Susie even asked me to apologize to Bob for stepping on his toe.

I figured this had gone far enough and told Bob he needed to stay at Susie's house from now on and not come back to school. It was funny watching her interacting with the other students like a real person was there, but I couldn't laugh. All I could do was watch the fun from a distance!

Christmas came so quickly that first year. I was learning how to be a teacher just like the children were learning the math I presented to them. Finally we would have some time to celebrate together and have fun. I was allowed to read the Christmas story from the Bible and also to answer questions the children had about the true meaning of Christmas. I cherished those moments and thanked God that the opportunities were there for them to hear from God's Word. It wasn't long before those privileges were taken away and the Bible could no longer be used in the classroom.

We made ornaments and wrote stories about Christmas. We had art projects related to Christmas hanging in the hallway. We were ready for the last day before our break when our class would celebrate with snacks, games, gifts, and songs all day. The children came into the room that morning laden with gifts, cookies, and candy. I had prepared a table for the food, so they stopped to relieve their burden before arriving at my desk with their gift for me.

The children stood all around my desk, waiting for me to open their gifts. I opened gifts that ranged from gift cards to nice restaurants in Oxford, to earrings, to small figurines from the dollar store, and finally to a large dress box full of homemade candy and cookies.

Sonia stood back and watched as I opened the gifts from the other children. She held a small, crudely wrapped present in her hand and waited until all the other children had walked away. She slowly handed the present to me and said, "Merry Christmas, Mrs. Carter. I made this for you."

I opened the present with the same enthusiasm I had shown the other students and with anticipation for what Sonia created. As I opened the lid of the box, I saw a beautiful beaded ornament in the shape of a star. The beads were in pastel colors, and the ornament was delicately made.

I hugged her neck and told her how beautiful the ornament was. I thanked her for spending the time to make this gift and told her it would be very special to me. She looked at me and said, "Reedy Acres only had enough beads to make two ornaments. I made this one for you, and I made the other one for my mother when she comes back to get me. I will keep it safe until then."

The smile that appeared on her face broke my heart. I couldn't keep the tears from falling. Sonia wedged a place in my heart that would remain forever. I still pray for her even though I have no idea where she is today. I just pray that she has found the Lord and is happy.

I taught for four wonderful years in Water Valley. The students were a blessing, and the teachers became close friends. However, I wanted to be closer to home, so I decided in the spring of 2003 to apply at the Lafayette County School District (again) and see if I could get a job there. I prayed about this decision and knew I was making the right choice.

I submitted my application and was called for an interview. This time around I was able to go alone to the interview. After a year of voice therapy following my embolism, I was able to speak normally. This time, I also had teaching experience. I walked into the interview with Mr. Herod and was hired to teach fourth grade.

I had just begun my fifth year of teaching. I was now in a small class of sixteen students at Lafayette Elementary School. Even in the first few days of school, I could see God's hand working.

I walked into the counselor's office on the second day of school, only to find out that a child had been moved out of my classroom. His dad had been transferred, and he would soon start school in a different state. While I was talking with the counselor, I heard a small voice from behind me say, "Mama, there's Mrs. Carter." I turned around, and there stood a precious little blond-headed boy. He was grinning from ear to ear, but I didn't recognize him.

His mom asked him where he might know me from. The child looked at his mom and said, "Oh Mom, Mrs. Carter teaches in Water Valley."

I explained to them that I was now teaching in the Lafayette District in the fourth grade. Then in turn, the mom told me that her son was transferring from Water Valley to Lafayette and would be in the fourth grade.

The counselor heard our conversation and asked the child if he would like to fill the slot in my class that had just been opened. He started to clap and jump up and down.

The mom later told me that the child's dad had been deployed to Iraq. The child had been suffering from depression and sleeplessness just worrying about his dad. He had also been afraid of attending a different school.

She said, "I have been praying that he would have a teacher who would love him and understand his situation, and I feel like you are an answer to my prayer." Needless to say, I wanted to cry, but all I could do was praise an almighty God who loves us enough to plan our future.

I found that all children are basically alike. They need to feel secure and loved, and they want to learn, especially when their different learning styles are acknowledged. They want to be accepted for the people they are, not who you want them to be.

Every day when I walked into my classroom I knew God was standing right beside me. I knew He would never leave me and that I was in that classroom because of His divine plan for me.

As a reminder of His presence, I wrote a letter and posted it near my desk in my classroom. This was the first thing that I saw when I sat at my desk in the morning.

Dear Carolyn,

I've started a good work in you. When you feel overwhelmed and at the end of your rope, look up and remember that your help comes from Me. Please don't lose heart in doing good, for in My perfect timing, I promise you will see a reward if you don't give up. Be confident that I will faithfully complete the things I have birthed in you.

> With everlasting
> love,
> Your heavenly Father

# CHAPTER 16

# THE PUZZLE OF MY LIFE

As a child, I thought life was perfect. I didn't have a care in the world, and my only real sadness came when my mother told me I needed to stay home instead of going to a friend's house to play. I was born into a wonderful Christian home, complete with loving parents who provided for my every need. I had an older brother I looked up to, and I wanted to pattern my life after his. We lived in a beautiful home my grandfather had built with his own hands.

I was a very shy child in a very adult-filled world. Daddy was elected mayor of the city of Oxford when I was just five years old. I didn't understand what that meant at the time, but I knew that I was around more and more adults as the years went by. I was constantly being nudged by my mother and reminded to talk to their friends. It was really intimidating to be the timid child of friendly, outgoing parents who seemed to know everyone on this earth.

At that time, my life was a blank slate. I really thought the puzzle pieces of my life had begun to be put together to form what I would become and would be someday. The years of growing were developing my body, educating my mind, and shaping my personality. However, I didn't realize that this was not true until I was thirteen years old and for the first time realized that I needed Jesus our Lord and Savior as a part of my life.

After accepting Jesus, I began to realize that God would work through my life to complete His plan and purpose for my presence here on earth. As I began to grow older, I also became aware that prayer is not a spare tire to be pulled out in times of trouble but is really the steering wheel that directs our path through our lifetime. God already knows our hearts but cherishes the personal time with us.

It was during this time that my recurring prayer began: "God, grant me the courage to share my faith with others. Take away the fear of rejection so I will feel bold enough to share Your love with other people." I prayed this prayer daily for many years.

I didn't realize how God was beginning to put the puzzle pieces together in my life. When we go through the problems of life, sometimes we are so close to a problem that we are unable to see a clear solution. All we can see is the problem and the whirlwind in our lives that it causes. But once we step outside the box of life, we can see that God was walking beside us all along.

I went to college and made a conscious decision to become a new person in a new world. I lived on campus and joined a sorority. I made tons of new friends and had fun becoming the outgoing person I had always wanted to be. As I look back, it's easy to see the perception my high school friends and family had. Our personalities are formed when we are children, and good or bad, it is difficult to break out of that mold. However, I was determined to do it and start a new life with all of my new friends.

I prayed and trusted that God would give me the strength to become the new person He could use without the timid, shy personality. It worked! Gary wouldn't believe that I grew up as an introverted, shy person. He questioned many of my childhood friends, who reassured him that I really had come out of my shy shell.

God began putting together those beautiful puzzle pieces of my life during my college years as He used me to talk with others about

Christ. He put me through trials that I realized later were to build my character and help others to believe.

He placed Gary in my life and gave me a reason to pray and believe that miracles do happen. I prayed that God would give me the characteristics that Gary needed to see in a true Christian. On the day Gary accepted Christ as his Savior, God placed a beautiful piece into the puzzle of my life. He gave me a wonderful husband who cherished our marriage as much as I did.

Probably the most unusual puzzle piece was created when my three-year-old son innocently admired the shiny diamonds in my cross and allowed a thief to make his plan. Even a novelist couldn't have written a more complex story that would bring an innocent young lady into my business, allow me to be the one to help her and recognize my cross around her neck, and then use a drunkard to apprehend the thief. Just one last note about this awesome story: when Jerry was let out of jail on bond, he went to his house and called his girlfriend. When she arrived, Jerry had been drinking in celebration of his release and was quite drunk. She did go to visit, but no one will ever know exactly what was said behind those closed doors. Jerry died that night when his house went up in flames.

When Chris was born, I loved my job as a mom. Chris was such a blessing and the joy of our life. I realized that I would need to depend on God for protection for this active child to keep him safe. Chris's childhood was a time when God added many pieces to my puzzle as I depended on Him more and more through prayer and a listening ear. As Chris grew older and went through a troubled stage in his life, I felt as though God was not there. I would call out to Him but could not feel His presence. But I thanked Him anyway for keeping Chris safe and opening up opportunities to help Chris.

I began to realize that God was working out a plan for Chris when $16,500 showed up out of the blue and allowed His plan to be complete. I was so close to the problem that I was unable to see that God was with us all the way. He was providing the path and walking beside us through our entire journey.

This journey proved to be the turning point in Chris's life that has made him the man of character and respect that he is today. Today Chris remains the pride and joy of my life, along with his beautiful family. I was so close to the problem that I couldn't see that God was painting that puzzle piece and preparing it for my puzzle of life.

God asked Gary and me to sell the jewelry store to free our commitments for the coming months and redirect our lives. Gary was able to stay at home and take care of me after my accident, which would not have been possible if we had still owned the store. During that time, I learned how to be more patient and understanding of others. I also learned how life feels when confined to a wheelchair. After my experiences, human life was more precious to me. I was able to see the hearts of others more clearly and show compassion where there had been none.

God also was taking care of us in an economic time that would have been devastating to our business. Our business was strong and healthy, but God knew that if we stayed there, the business would not remain that way. Through the years, we have seen many nonessential enterprises go out of business. The grocery stores, car repair shops, doctors' offices, and Wal-Mart stores are still doing well, but who can't live without jewelry? When something has to be cut from the budget, it will not be groceries or gas. It will be nonessential items like jewelry and expensive gifts. Thank you, God, for being our eyes into the future.

God used my broken legs as a starting point to reach many lives. Even as an invalid, He was preparing me to be the messenger I had prayed to be and getting me ready to share His Word and miracles with others throughout the world. As my broken legs gave way to a pulmonary embolism, Gary began to send e-mails to friends to pray for me. These friends sent Gary's e-mail to other friends. The chain of e-mails reached to the remotest parts of the world and before long, people I had never met were praying in Singapore, Canada, the Bahamas, Japan, and throughout the United States.

These prayers were answered by my life being restored and God's miracle being acknowledged by all. On that Sunday night, I had the privilege to become one of the very few to be accepted into God's presence and then come back to His earthly kingdom to share my faith with others.

I later realized that God had answered my lifelong prayer on Sunday, June 6, 1999. I had prayed to be able to share the Word of God with a commitment that would help others see His love in my life. Many times I had read 2 Timothy 1:7-8 NASB, which says, "For God has not given us a spirit of timidity, but of power and love and discipline. Therefore do not be ashamed of the testimony of our Lord or of me His prisoner, but join with me in suffering for the gospel according to the power of God." I was not ashamed of knowing and loving our Lord Jesus Christ. I had been afraid of having to accept rejection that I might receive for proclaiming His name to others.

His miracles and answered prayers in my life have allowed me to be bold in my faith. Others were brought to know Christ through the miracle in my life. God answered my prayer, "God, give me the strength to share Your Word."

That was not the way I expected Him to use me, but I am truly thankful He did. I would go through that miracle again if more could come to understand the joy that only Christ can give. The puzzle piece of miracles was truly a turning point in my life.

I thank God for every blessing and every trial in my life. Without trials in our lives, we can't learn how to become really dependent on God. If we listen, God will teach us how to handle future problems and praise Him for His protection. How wonderful it is to know that our lives have a plan that can include protection and provision with God or struggles and battles without God.

My puzzle is not yet complete. How wonderful it is that we don't know our future. Only God knows. I just pray that when the puzzle is complete and I stand in His presence, God will say, "My good and faithful servant. You were faithful with a few things, I will put you in charge of many things; enter into the joy of your master" (Matt. 25:23 NASB).

CPSIA information can be obtained at www.ICGtesting.com
Printed in the USA
LVOW040754010312

270977LV00001B/7/P